Leo Strauss

THE JOHNS HOPKINS SERIES

IN CONSTITUTIONAL THOUGHT

Sanford Levinson & Jeffrey K. Tulis,

Series Editors

Leo Strauss

AN INTRODUCTION TO HIS

THOUGHT AND INTELLECTUAL

LEGACY **Thomas L. Pangle**

The Johns Hopkins University Press BALTIMORE

© 2006 The Johns Hopkins University Press
All rights reserved. Published 2006
Printed in the United States of America on acid-free paper

9 8 7 6 5 4 3 2 1

The Johns Hopkins University Press
2715 North Charles Street
Baltimore, Maryland 21218-4363
www.press.jhu.edu

Library of Congress Cataloging-in-Publication Data
Pangle, Thomas L.
Leo Strauss : an introduction to his thought and
intellectual legacy / Thomas L. Pangle.
p. cm.
Includes bibliographical references and index.
ISBN 0-8018-8439-x (hardcover : alk. paper) —
ISBN 0-8018-8440-3 (pbk. : alk. paper)
1. Strauss, Leo. I. Title.
JC251.S8P36 2006
320.092—dc22
2006001442

A catalog record for this book is available from
the British Library.

Contents

Acknowledgments

I thank the Social Sciences and Humanities Research Council of Canada, as well as the National Endowment for the Humanities of the United States, and the Earhart Foundation, for grant support, which allowed me the time off from teaching during which I did much of the work on this book. I am also grateful for the help afforded by the research funds accompanying the Joe R. Long Chair in Democratic Studies at the University of Texas at Austin.

Earlier versions of parts of chapters two and three were presented as a Bradley Lecture, at the American Enterprise Institute in Washington, D.C., in December 2003, and appeared in Dutch translation as "Leo Strauss' visie op de moderne politiek," in *Nexus* 36 (2003), pp. 55–72, and then in the English original as "Leo Strauss's Perspective on Modern Politics," *Perspectives on Political Science* 25:4 (Fall, 2004).

An earlier and much shorter version of chapter four was published as "Straussian Approaches to the Study of Politics," in Gerald F. Gaus and Chandran Kukathas, eds., *Handbook of Political Theory* (London: Sage Publications, 2004), 31–45.

I am grateful to Johns Hopkins University Press series editor Jeffrey Tulis for suggesting this volume and even more for his persistent and most insightful and constructive criticisms and exhortations.

Leo Strauss

Introduction

As the years pass that slowly but steadily distance us from the lifetime of Leo Strauss (1899–1973), his thought grows into the future with a reach and significance rivaled by very few of his twentieth-century contemporaries. This is the case precisely because Strauss's philosophic enterprise does not express, is not at home in—does not even unambiguously belong to—the twentieth century. Strauss exemplifies Nietzsche's observation that genuinely independent thinkers are never the "children of their times": they are (at most) the subversive and rebellious, the despised or decried, the troublesome and trouble-making "stepchildren" of their times. Their reflections come to sight as more than merely disturbing or thought provoking. To the upholders of the conventionally respectable intellectual norms, a maverick like Strauss—with his insistent and abrasive questioning of so much that is held to be "unquestionable"—looms up as outrageous and alien, even downright frightening.

Yet despite this common reaction, it is becoming increasingly evident (to the bewildered consternation of those who warm themselves at the fires of the various orthodoxies of Left and Right) that Strauss's iconoclastic writings have long exercised a profound subterranean cultural influence,[1] which is now emerging more and more into broad daylight, especially among the rising younger generation. The captivating power of Strauss's complex thought is seen at least as much outside the cloistered academy as within: markedly in America, but also abroad, in the East (near and far) as well as across continental Europe, most prominently in France and Germany. Starting in the spring of 2003, the "highbrow" media in Europe, and then in North America, awoke to the widespread impact of Strauss or of "Straussians," among all sorts of weighty circles in and outside of government. The media suddenly discovered the powerful undertow that can be quietly exercised by authentic philosophic reflection. In a curious contagion of speculative excitement, American journalists and intellectuals, especially on the Left, reacted with a febrile flurry of conspiracy theories. They traced their bêtes noires—the Bush "neoconservative" domestic as well as foreign policies—to Strauss's purportedly malignant and demonic shaping influence, reaching out from the grave through numerous supposedly mesmerized disciples.[2]

On the other hand, and partly in response, major voices in the German and the French press, and at least one influential French Straussian writing provocatively in a leading American journal, suggested that Strauss's thought had been "betrayed," or put to distorted use, by his powerful American followers in the Bush administration: Strauss's genuine legacy, these defenders contended, was the upholding of the spirit of "old Europe" against or in the face of the "hegemony of the USA."[3]

The chief good that might have resulted from this mildly hysterical media flurry could have been the spurring of some to a serious investigation of Strauss's writings. Unfortunately, however, this salutary consequence was not much in evidence among those in the United States who pronounced vociferously about Strauss in print.[4] The conspiracy theorists proceeded to invent increasingly extravagant (and even preposterous) claims about what Strauss thought or taught. These fabulous concoctions were marked by their lack of substantiation through genuine quotations from, or even through accurate summaries of, anything to be found in Strauss's numerous and widely circulating publications. Words were placed in quotation marks, to be sure, but on inspection the quotes all turned out to be from journalists and others claiming to report what Strauss was thought to have thought; the quotations (when the phrases were not invented out of whole cloth or ripped out of context and pasted together)[5] were never quotations from Strauss. This is, I think, a kind of unintended testimonial tribute to the nature of Strauss's political theorizing. For this remarkable inability of the sensationalists to come up with genuine quotations from any of Strauss's many publications indicates the moderation and the civic responsibility that characterizes Strauss's theorizing —despite or indeed because of that theorizing's philosophic radicalism. Various commentators can of course think up all sorts of dramatic or scary things to say about what Strauss is purported to have thought or written; but they just cannot find any statements of his to quote (or to quote with any reasonable accuracy) in order to substantiate their ominous attributions.

The commotion in the media made clearer than ever before the need for, and the absence of, an accurate, brief, and nonpolemical introduction to Strauss's mature thought and intellectual legacy. This is what I hope to provide in the present book. I mean to open a pathway that may guide serious inquirers toward Strauss's highly controversial central themes and concerns. In presenting and interpreting Strauss's thought, I will speak as much as possible in the terms and even in the very words of Strauss himself, doing so with a meticulous attention to the authentic context of whatever I quote. I will not attempt anything like a thorough interpretation of his oeuvre as a whole, or even of any of his major works. Instead, I will offer a guide to Strauss's writings that approaches them from the perspective of an attempt to begin to answer the question of their significance for our understanding of the deeply problematic roots of the contemporary political world in which we find ourselves historically situated.

This is the sort of question that is perhaps most likely to bring readers who hear about Strauss to a sustained interest in learning more about him; and it seems to me that this kind of serious, civic-minded curiosity deserves a thoughtful response. At the same time, I must start with a word of caution, precisely on this point. For this is an avenue of approach that is fraught with hazards of distortion and self-delusion or spiritual self-impoverishment—both for those who defend or promote Strauss, and for those who attack or decry him and his influence. When we insist on addressing to Strauss solely or even chiefly the questions and demands that arise from our immediate and partisan contemporary political passions, we run the grave risk of shoehorning Strauss's subtle reflections into our predetermined categories, which function like a Procrustean bed that wrenches beyond recognition the living body that has been manacled upon it. Having made Strauss's corpus the victim of our ham-handed interrogation, we are all too likely to destroy the very possibility of listening to, and thereby of learning something of the greatest importance from, what he is trying to tell us. We may close ourselves off from, rather than opening ourselves up to, the possibility that our concerns — despite, or indeed because of, the intensity with which we feel them — are not in truth the most serious or even the most urgent concerns that ought to preoccupy us. We may miss the opportunity to discover that the most important thing that we have to learn from a candid encounter with Strauss is above all our way back to the truly most urgent and serious issues that have been buried from our sight.

Unfortunately, these dangers have substantially materialized in much or most of what has been written about Strauss thus far, by some of those who have sought to rescue Strauss from abuses of his name as well as by those who have tried to paint him as a Mephistophelean influence behind what they hate or fear. As a consequence, my own discussion, in what follows, has been unavoidably colored or bent by the necessity of trying to counter, implicitly as well as explicitly, some of the most widespread and gross of the misunderstandings that have tended to blight the discussions of Strauss's thought.

But it is not only Strauss's own writing and thought that have been transmogrified in recent popularizing accounts. Strauss's influence — especially as exercised through diverse intellectuals and academics who follow his lead closely enough to be labeled (often pejoratively) "Straussians" — has been portrayed in polemical terms so narrow and counterfeit as to be ludicrous. As the months have passed since the first media flurry, the increasingly embarrassed confession, or embarrassing exposure, of the idiocies perpetrated in the media concerning Strauss's own thought has led to a new gambit: Strauss himself, it is now admitted, was of course a great thinker (even if no one can take the time to figure him out); the problem is, his American followers have all grossly misappropriated and distorted his teaching.

Now no doubt Strauss, like every fertile thinker, has attracted his share of foolish enthusiasts and exploitative appropriators. It is also true that, as is to be expected, earnest scholars who attempt to follow his lead exhibit a range, the low end of which embarrasses his name, and even the top echelon of which rarely rises to his own extraordinary level. But these justified critical observations only limn the fact that there now exists a very substantial and far-ranging body of scholarship and journalism inspired, in varying degrees, by Strauss, which sets and meets a high civic and intellectual standard. One contributing reason for this, apart from the help Strauss's guidance affords, is the situation in which many or most of the intellectuals inspired in varying degrees and ways by Strauss find themselves. They are an embattled and dispersed minority. Their work relentlessly challenges the most fundamental, late-modern, intellectual conventions and commitments that tend to form the consensus, even across secondary disagreements, of the vast majority of their colleagues. Where these latter see "progress," the followers of Strauss see a growing forgetfulness of the most important questions that once preoccupied the greatest minds. Since the "Straussians" constantly "cause trouble" by voicing this animadversion, since they do not cease to expose what they regard as the dubious grounds of what their colleagues hold to be intellectually settled or even sacrosanct, those influenced by Strauss cannot avoid constantly incurring and being forced to confront a most stimulating counterchallenge—consisting in at least the widespread authoritative opinion that they are wrong, morally as well as intellectually, in voicing such seemingly old-fashioned or out-of-the-mainstream criticisms. This reaction, encountered on every side, constantly forces those so criticized to rethink, in order to defend (first and foremost before their own intellectual consciences), the justifying foundations of their out-of-step or even disreputable positions.

To be sure, by placing themselves in so intellectually aggressive, and consequently embattled or isolated, a salient, those conspicuously influenced by Strauss may incur the danger of slipping into a defensiveness that can perhaps distort thinking, as well as impinge upon collegiality; but this is a cost well worth paying in return for the invigorating pressure to self-questioning and to intellectual probity. Strauss himself never ceased to stress that a truly vital intellectual life is a life of controversy, of intense argument. He concluded his most public presentation—the Walgreen Lectures that later became the book *Natural Right and History*—with the remark: "It has been well said of Aristotle, '*Solet Aristoteles quaerere pugnam*'; 'Aristotle has a habit of seeking a fight.' He is seeking a fight not because he loves fight and enmity but because he loves peace and friendship; but true peace and friendship can only be found in the truth." The Aristotelian "seeking of a fight" as the way to the truth sometimes produces among "Straussians" an irritatingly quixotic scorn for the ordinary avenues and polite niceties of career advancement; but this is a risk that attends the liberating habit of thinking along avenues that are not "respectable"—of venturing deep into questions that are intensely "unpopular" and, in an intellectual sense, subversive.

In my last chapter I offer a bibliographic survey of a limited portion of this wide-ranging and diverse, often sharply conflicting, body of scholarship that embodies and conveys what is Strauss's most massive intellectual legacy thus far. I stress that I survey only a limited portion. I have not attempted to canvass the multitude of writings that continue and extend Strauss's own work, in political philosophy and in the history of political philosophy. I have made reference to such work only when it is directly related to my restricted and lowered focus, which is rather on writings that exhibit the extension of Strauss's influence into the more "practical," "empirical," subphilosophic fields of social and political science and commentary. I mean to offer what is an unavoidably cursory and incomplete (a necessarily selective, and thus contestably subjective), but I hope nevertheless useful, orientation to this major aspect of Strauss's legacy, as practiced and as contributed to by numerous scholars and teachers (and also by a few journalists and commentators). These analysts of the contemporary world, and of its roots and its presuppositions, have taken Strauss's impulse into large areas in which Strauss himself did not personally or at least directly venture. Thus my final chapter on Strauss's legacy continues and extends this book's response to the question: what does Strauss's thinking have to contribute to today's civic self-understanding and renewal?

eo Strauss's writings consist mostly of interpretative commentaries on the works of major thinkers of past ages. Strauss thus comes to sight as a scholar of the history of thought. But he utterly transforms the meaning, the scope, and the significance of such study. His meticulous textual interpretations are intended to show that there are a few key books and authors from the past that should be studied as sources of powerful, even though clashing, claims to wisdom. These comprehensive teachings and their titanic disagreements, he contends, we today desperately need to try to fathom, to revivify, and to bring into strenuous debate—with a view to our judging among them. For as regards the pressing ultimate questions of human existence—What is the good life? What is the right or just way to live? What is the fulfilling purpose of human existence?— we in the late-modern West have lost our bearings, Strauss insists: and to such an abysmal extent that we are in the process of becoming bereft of even the capacity to seriously pursue the quest for answers.

No doubt, we continue in some degree to share, and even heroically to defend, what we call "our basic common values." But the very expression "our values" signals the deep problem. Under the influence of our most prestigious intellectual authorities, we no longer confidently believe in the rationally demonstrable, universal, and permanent truth of the principles, purposes, and way of life that we share and defend. Still worse, or more fundamentally, we gravely doubt the very possibility that any principles, any purposes, any way of life can be shown by reason to be simply true: that is, truly right, truly good, for all humanity as such.[1] We have become more and more resigned to the view that all evaluation and all basis for evaluation is irretrievably rooted in and limited by the deeply discordant, rationally inadjudicable "perspectives" of the diverse historical "cultures" or "worldviews" or "faiths" of the specific human beings doing the evaluating.[2] Increasingly we find ourselves clinging to and asserting "our Western, liberal values" over and against alien, contrary "values" for no reason at bottom beyond the historical fate that has made them ours.

Yet our specific culture—the modernity that culminates in the liberal and democratic West—has always defined itself and its highest purpose or object of dedication in universal and rational terms. Ours is the culture of "humanism" and of humanity's "enlightenment," to and through reason or rationalism. From the beginning, modernity has championed the liberation of mankind, as a whole, from traditional, parochial "superstitions" and "prejudices." Our culture has prided itself on being rooted in the objective normative truth for and about all of humanity: the "natural rights" of man, the "palpable truth" disclosed by reason or "the light of science."[3] It follows that this culture of ours cannot lose faith in reason, as the ground for universally evident and valid human norms discoverable in nature or human nature, without losing faith in itself, in its very core. As a consequence, we inhabit a culture slipping into spiritual disintegration and bewilderment (CM, 3).

Strauss does not hesitate to characterize this spiritual situation as "the crisis of our times," or "the contemporary crisis of the West." He stresses that we are confronted everywhere today with severe doubts as to the status of the specific, comprehensive conception of the collective and individual purpose of humanity that, up through the first half of the twentieth century, explicitly animated and guided the modern Western nations in their apparently intensifying global leadership. This universal purpose "we find expressly stated," Strauss notes (CM, 3–4), "in our immediate past, for instance in famous official declarations made during the two World Wars." "These declarations," Strauss adds, "merely restate the purpose stated originally by the most successful form of modern political philosophy." Strauss summarizes the Enlightenment philosophers' statements of purpose, using their own phraseology, as follows:[4] "philosophy or science was no longer to be understood as essentially contemplative and proud but as active and charitable"; "it was to enable man to become the master and owner of nature through the intellectual conquest of nature." Science, thus radically transformed, "should make possible progress toward ever greater prosperity," and "thus enable everyone to share in all the advantages of society or life and therewith give full effect" to "everyone's natural right to develop all his faculties fully in concert with everyone else's doing the same." This "progress toward ever greater prosperity would thus become, or render possible, the progress toward ever greater freedom and justice." This "would necessarily be the progress toward a society embracing equally all human beings: a universal league of free and equal nations, each nation consisting of free and equal men and women." For "it had come to be believed that," in order to "make the world safe for the Western democracies, one must make the whole globe democratic, each country in itself as well as the society of nations."

By the second half of the twentieth century, Strauss submits, "this view of the human situation in general and of the situation in our century in particular" no longer "retains plausibility." The most obvious, if not the most profound, reason is that the once supposedly triumphant West has undergone shattering experiences. We have witnessed in the very bosom of the West horrifying totalitarian police states based on slave labor and on mass exterminations —all engineered by a science under the tutelage of fantastic ideological faiths and dreams. The same science, which has proven to be compatible with all sorts of mutually hostile secular and religious extremism, continues to enable and even to inspire ghastly international races to invent and build weapons of mass destruction. Looming over us is the specter of increasing environmental destruction, and before us gleams the lurid dawn of genetic manipulation. Within us we feel the spiritual vacuum—even the guilt —left by the recognition of our loss of reverence for nature as a whole as well as for human nature in particular. These experiences have instilled or resuscitated a pervasive sense of unease and fear in the face of the ungovernable power that technology places in the hands of a human race that seems in no whit morally improved or even morally enlightened by its acquisition of domination over nature.

At the same time, late-modern science has ever more explicitly discovered and proclaimed of itself—and of reason or rationality altogether—that it is constitutionally incapable of offering to humanity any ultimate guidance as to how the ever increasing power that science brings into being is to be used rather than abused. Late-modern science has sternly announced that it judges, and that it is only competent to judge, "facts" not "values"—the "Is" not the "Ought." Science of course has to be directed by "values," by someone's "oughts"; but science as science cannot provide or validate the ultimate values that must direct it. Our science "may make us very wise or clever as regards the means for any objectives we might choose. It admits to being unable to help us in discriminating between legitimate and illegitimate, between just and unjust, objectives. Such a science is instrumental and nothing but instrumental: it is born to be the handmaid of any powers or any interests that be. . . . According to our social science, we can be or become wise in all matters of secondary importance, but we have to be resigned to utter ignorance in the most important respect: we cannot have any knowledge regarding the ultimate principles of our choices" (NRH, 4).

Late-modern science, as the supposedly most perfected form of the rational comprehension of human experience, looks upon political philosophy's claim to discover grounds for basic norms in nature or in the rationality of the historical process as a manifestation of grave misunderstanding of the scope and capacity of reason's analysis of experience or of "the empirical." Early-modern liberal political philosophy's original normative appeal to human nature (that is, to "natural right" or "natural rights") is regarded no longer as science, but rather as "ideology"—meaning to say, some sort of "constructed," nonverifiable, quasi-mythic interpretation imposed upon or manipulative of the human phenomena. Science may show that humans cannot live without one or another such ideology structuring their existence; science certainly lends to any of the conflicting actual ideologies very great powers; but to which ideology *ought* science to lend, and to which *ought* it to refuse, its powers? That question seeks an answer that is beyond the ken of the scientist as scientist. That, we are told, is not a scientific question. As Strauss puts it: through the power given by science, "modern man is a giant in comparison to earlier man"; but, given the nature of late-modern science in relation to norms, one must add that insofar as this giant is "scientific" or is scientifically rational, there is no escaping the coda: "modern man is a blind giant" (RCPR, 239).

Late-modern science unquestionably generates increasing economic prosperity and even, eventually, affluence. But, to say the least, "there is no corresponding increase in wisdom and goodness." In the so-called developed nations, we now have considerable experience of prosperity and affluence. That very experience— not least the way the "underdeveloped nations" have been treated by the "developed"—has made the West "doubtful of the belief that affluence is the sufficient and even necessary condition of happiness and justice: affluence does not cure the deepest evils" (RCPR, 239, and CM, 6).

On the more strictly political level, it has become evident that the urge to homogenize mankind and to unify the globe politically, even or especially on democratic premises, carries with it a new and unprecedented version of the threat of imperialism, and indeed of universal despotism—and not necessarily merely Tocqueville's "soft despotism" of paternalistic bureaucracy ruling a herdlike and childlike humanity. The far harsher threat of the late-modern will to power has appeared most starkly in the reach for permanent terrestrial dominance by the Marxist-inspired Soviet Union, with the resultant Cold War.[5]

The experience of Communism, Strauss suggests, taught a deep and broad lesson. In its radical egalitarianism, in its thirst for technological "development" and accompanying economic growth and universal prosperity, in its aspiration to "liberate" all of mankind from everything "unscientific" or "irrational," in its historical-materialist progressivism and secularism, or its unqualified hope that mankind's deepest problems and longings could find a worldly, historical solution and satisfaction—above all, in its moral insistence on sacrificing everything to this ultimate common good of secular humanity or humanism, Communism confronted the West like a kind of nightmare sibling. For "it was impossible for the Western movement to understand Communism as merely a new version of that eternal reactionism against which it had been fighting for centuries." "From the Communist Manifesto it would appear that the victory of Communism would be the complete victory of the West—of the synthesis, transcending the national boundaries, of British industry, the French Revolution, and German philosophy." But Communism in fact was a monstrosity, whose monstrousness had to be recognized as no mere accident. The confrontation with Communism allowed or compelled the modern West to confront something deeply problematic and inadequate in itself, in its own project and fundamental principles.

For some time, and in many quarters, "it seemed sufficient to say that while the Western movement agrees with Communism regarding the goal—the universal prosperous society of free and equal men and women—it disagrees with it regarding the means." But slowly it became clear that the disagreement over means was a disagreement over a core dimension of human existence—a dimension that cannot, however, be adequately understood or expressed on the basis of modern rationalism. From the perspective of "Communism, the end, the common good of the whole human race, being the most sacred thing, justifies any means." Nay, "whatever contributes to the achievement of the most sacred end partakes of its sacredness and is therefore itself sacred"; and by the same token, "whatever hinders the achievement of that end is devilish." Seeing what this meant, in action, compelled the liberal West to recoil, in a kind of abashed self-discovery: "it came to be seen that there is not only a difference of degree but of kind between the Western movement and Communism, and this difference was seen to concern morality, the choice of means." For the Western movement, in opposition to Communism, the choice of means is not and cannot be decided solely by the answer to the question of what will most efficiently promote the goal that is shared with Communism. That goal—"the universal prosperous society of free and equal men and women"—does not adequately capture what the West still experiences as morally sacred, as placing sacred limits on human striving, even on the striving for universal freedom and prosperity.

The liberal West was impelled to rediscover something that may be said to be of supreme and abiding, if sometimes hidden, importance for all humans in all times and places—something that had never ceased to be at work within the modern West, but that could not be adequately recognized or articulated by the modern Western principles, even in their most moralistic (Kantian) version. For what the modern West rediscovered was the natural human concern with political good and evil that cannot be explained in terms of the human quest for, and understanding or misunderstanding of, rational power and freedom or autonomy. The evil manifested in Communism was at its core a perverted or fanatic expression of this natural and inevitable civic concern for the sacred, which includes a sacrificial civic duty or call to identify and to fight, as evil, as devilish, that which always threatens the sacred; and this means to say that the natural concern for the sacred is a permanently high and mighty source of antagonistic political diversity. The experience and the expression of good and evil as it thus characterizes human nature cannot be expected to dwindle away in the course of—instead, it can explosively take over—the apparently ever more enlightened march toward universal freedom and prosperity. This, I believe, is what Strauss has in mind when he writes that, from the experience of Communism, "in other words, it became clearer than it had been for some time that no bloody or unbloody change of society can eradicate the evil in man: as long as there will be men, there will be malice, envy and hatred."

On the politically temporary level, the Cold War compelled the liberal West to recognize that "even if one would still contend that the Western purpose is as universal as the Communist, one must rest satisfied for the foreseeable future with a practical particularism." But as this wording suggests, Strauss sees the West as being forced to wonder, at the level of principle, whether one could still contend that the West should aim at a purpose as universal as the Communist. Has not the confrontation with the evil of Communism, has not the rediscovery of the sacred and its perversions—the rediscovery of good and evil in their full meaning—made it necessary to qualify or to moderate, by recognizing the incompleteness of, the liberal principles themselves? Hence Strauss immediately adds: "the situation resembles the one which existed during the centuries in which Christianity and Islam each raised its universal claim but had to be satisfied with uneasily coexisting with its antagonist." But "all this amounts to saying," Strauss concludes, "that for the foreseeable future, political society remains what it has always been: a partial or particular society whose most urgent and primary task is self-preservation and whose highest task is self-improvement"; and "as for the meaning of self-improvement, we may observe that the same experience which has made the West doubtful of the viability of a world-society has made it doubtful of the belief that affluence is the sufficient and even necessary condition of happiness and justice."

This analysis of the late-modern West's confrontation with radical evil, instantiated obviously in Communism, and of the attendant glimpses of the possibility of basic truths about the human condition that draw into question the adequacy of modern liberal political universalism and rationalism, begins to help us to understand the peculiar depth and unprecedented nature of the contemporary spiritual crisis of the West. For if or insofar as we become penetrated by the suspicion that modern liberal rationalism and political universalism must be tempered, regulated, governed, by some higher norms or standards, we confront the question: can *reason* supply such standards or norms? Is there —and if so, where is there—a transliberal, transmodern normative rationalism that can fill this bill? Or do we here stand on the brink of the discovery of reason's limitations, of the inescapable ultimate partiality, hence dependency, and hence historical relativism, of reason? What is unprecedented about our culture's spiritual crisis, what makes it unlike any previous known cultural crisis, is our pervasive relativism—our attempted abandonment, growing somehow out of our having trusted to reason, of the possibility of reason's arriving at transcultural or transhistorical norms. This attempted abandonment constitutes a new, never before seen, way of trying to understand our humanity that, Strauss contends, stifles self-critical thinking, and unconsciously promotes a passive conformism—doing so more effectively than any other way of thinking that has appeared in history.[6]

Strauss outlines the deeper[7] meaning, for us Americans, of historical or cultural relativism in the Introduction to his most synoptic book, *Natural Right and History.* That work opens with a solemn invocation of the Declaration of Independence's proclamation of the "self-evident truths" that "all men are created equal, that they are endowed by their Creator with certain unalienable Rights, that among these are Life, Liberty, and the pursuit of Happiness." Strauss goes on to observe that "the nation dedicated to this proposition has now become, no doubt partly as a consequence of this dedication, the most powerful and prosperous of the nations of the earth." Having thus reminded us of the enormous practical, or indeed existential, importance for America of its dedication to this proposition, Strauss raises trenchantly the question whether the nation in its maturity still cherishes "the faith in which it was conceived and raised." He proceeds to make clear how frail this "faith" in "natural rights" has become, and how deleterious are the consequences of this desuetude—due, he suggests, to the "imposing" on America of the alien "yoke" of "German thought,"[8] which "created the historical sense," and "thus was led eventually to unqualified relativism."

"The majority among the learned who still adhere to the principles of the Declaration of Independence," Strauss submits, "interpret these principles not as expressions of natural right but as an ideal, if not as an ideology or a myth."[9] What Strauss means in this context by the reduction of the principles of the Declaration of Independence to a mere "ideal" becomes clearer in the second paragraph, which Strauss begins by declaring that "the need for natural right is as evident today as it has been for centuries and even millennia." For "it is obviously meaningful, and sometimes even necessary, to speak of 'unjust' laws or 'unjust' decisions." And "in passing such judgments we imply that there is a standard of right and wrong independent of positive right and higher than positive right: a standard with reference to which we are able to judge of positive right." "Many people today hold the view" that "the standard of right and wrong" is "in the best case nothing but the ideal adopted by our society or our 'civilization' and embodied in its way of life or its institutions." Now "if principles are sufficiently justified by the fact that they are accepted by a society," then any and every society is equally justified in whatever it is dedicated to. Moreover, "if there is no standard higher than the ideal of our society, we are utterly unable to take a critical distance from that ideal." No one within "our" society has any ground other than personal preference for breaking allegiance to "us."[10] By the same token, no individual has any ground other than personal preference for espousing or remaining loyal to any ideal. But if personal preference is the highest standard for an individual, without a higher and fixed standard to which every individual preference ought to bow, then "everything a man is willing to dare will be permissible." If one asks, "what is there that puts moral limits on what any and all humans can will and do?"—the answer is: "nothing." And this is *nihilism* plain and simple: "the contemporary rejection of natural right leads to nihilism—nay, it is identical with nihilism."

Strauss thus commences the book by responding to, and encouraging in his readers, a strong patriotic hope mixed with or growing out of a sense of alarm. If or insofar as the disinterment of natural right from history or from historical relativism leads to a reinvigoration of the possibility of rationally reaffirming the truth of natural right, will this not contribute, not only to the overcoming of nihilism, but to the resuscitation of that specific "faith" that is the original, the inspiring and life-giving, dedication of the American nation? Moreover, by placing at the threshold of his discussion a dual long epigraph from the Bible (2 Samuel 12 and 1 Kings 21), Strauss responds to and encourages even further-reaching hopes: will there not be found an important connection between the Bible's teaching and the Lockean teaching of a rationally demonstrable "Creator" who has "endowed" all men with "certain unalienable Rights?"

Precisely if or because these hopes are truly strong, or express strength of soul, the hopes scorn to be coddled by illusions. Strauss thus continues to speak to these hopes when he signals in the fourth paragraph the deeply disconcerting complication. Despite the nihilistic outcome, "generous liberals" in America "view the abandonment of natural right not only with placidity but with relief." And this Strauss explains without further reference to "the yoke of German thought." This posture of "generous liberals" arises as a consequence of a "particular interpretation of natural right, according to which the one thing needful is respect for diversity or individuality." "*Liberal* relativism," Strauss finally declares, "has its roots in the natural right tradition of tolerance or in the notion that everyone has a natural right to the pursuit of happiness as he understands happiness."

But wait: is this not the very natural right tradition that finds expression in the previously quoted lapidary passage from the Declaration of Independence? Indeed. What then has happened, in history, to this tradition?

The original doctrine of natural rights—seen, in its classic form, we later hear (Chapter Five of NRH), in the treatises of John Locke above all—placed on the respect for individuality and diversity "absolute" limits. These limits were dictated by what were understood to be rational insights into natural (i.e., universal and unchanging) right or rights, as well as rational insights into what is by nature good and bad for human beings, in all times and places. From the very beginning, however, these claimed insights were accompanied by, or even based upon, prominent and emphatic denials that there exists anything that can be known to be *intrinsically* right, or anything that can be known to be *intrinsically* and universally—and not merely instrumentally or relatively—good or enjoyable.[11] It is this latter cornerstone of the original doctrine that provides the jumping-off point for the subsequent development. Today's "generous liberals," Strauss says, "appear to believe that our inability to acquire any genuine knowledge of what is intrinsically good or right compels us" to "recognize all preferences or all 'civilizations' as equally respectable." This compulsion, Strauss stresses, has been presented as a demand of reason: "only unlimited tolerance is in accordance with reason"; "all intolerant or all 'absolutist' positions" are "condemned because they are based on a demonstrably false premise, namely, that men can know what is good."

Yet this characterization of contemporary liberal relativism as an austere demand of reason does not get to the animating heart of the matter. For this does not explain the indignant "passion" with which "generous liberals" express their "condemnation" of "all 'absolutes.'" Liberal relativism is, paradoxically, a righteously censorious moralism. Strauss therefore adds: "at the bottom of the passionate rejection of all 'absolutes,' we discern the recognition of a natural right or, more precisely, of that particular interpretation of natural right according to which the one thing needful is respect for diversity or individuality." It is on the basis of this overriding imperative of respect for diversity or individuality that liberal relativists in effect claim a "rational or natural right" to "condemn" all "'absolutist' positions."

But, once it is made explicit, this particular version of rational or natural right stands exposed in its questionable coherence. "There is a tension between the respect for diversity or individuality and the recognition of natural right." For what about the many diverse cultures and individuals who are "absolutists," and even intolerant? On what ground do they, or the fervent and deeply held beliefs that define them, deserve less than equal respect? In other words, even "the most liberal version of natural right" turns out to contain at its heart an absolutism that excludes from equal respect the majority of humanity—all who are not liberal; all who do not embrace the tolerant, liberal notion of natural right.

The intellectual impasse, and the consequent astoundingly self-contradictory contortions, into which the recognition of this inescapable absolutism leads even or precisely intelligent and thoughtful liberal relativists Strauss illustrates in the case of his "famous contemporary," Isaiah Berlin. In Strauss's essay titled "Relativism," he focuses on Berlin's well-known monograph, *Two Concepts of Liberty*,[12] where Berlin attempts to provide a relativistic defense of the liberal idea of liberty and tolerance, in what Strauss terms "a characteristic document of the crisis of liberalism."

ISAIAH BERLIN AS PARADIGMATIC OF THE
DILEMMA OF LIBERAL RELATIVISTIC THEORY

Berlin defends what he calls the "negative" concept of liberty, or "freedom *from.*" Associated with thinkers like John Stuart Mill, this negative concept of liberty calls for (in Berlin's words) "a maximum degree of noninterference compatible with the minimum demands of social life." The threat to this latter liberty Berlin sees coming from what he calls the "positive" concept of liberty (or "freedom *to*")—associated with "Kant and the rationalists of his type." The positive concept of liberty requires that the individual "be his own master," or participate in the social control to which he is subject. This latter, positive concept of liberty is linked to the notion that true liberty is the liberation of a "true self," which is not the same as "our poor, desire-ridden, passionate, empirical selves."[13] Berlin spotlights, and his whole position is animated by his fear of, the danger that (as Strauss puts it in his paraphrase),[14] "positive freedom" has "to a higher degree the tendency to be understood as freedom only for the true self and therefore as compatible with the most extreme coercion of the empirical selves to become something that their true selves allegedly desire."

Yet Berlin admits and even stresses that negative liberty also requires that some minimal but strict coercive limits be placed on individual "freedom to live as one prefers." Strauss quotes the following words of Berlin: "there must be some frontiers of freedom which nobody should ever be permitted to cross"; those frontiers must be "absolute"—"Different names or natures may be given to the rules that determine these frontiers: they may be called natural rights or the word of God, or Natural law, or the demands of utility or of the 'deepest interests of man'; I may believe them to be valid a priori, or assert them to be my own subjective ends, or the ends of my society or culture. . . . Genuine belief in the inviolability of a minimum extent of individual liberty entails some such absolute stand" (Berlin, 1958: 50). Yes, but which stand? And what is the ground on which the liberal takes this stand? And how does he defend that ground rationally, with argument for and evidence of its validity? As Strauss protests, what Berlin is saying here is that "the demand for the sacredness of a private sphere needs a basis, an 'absolute' basis, but it has no basis; any old basis, any 'such absolute stand' as reference to my own subjective will or the will of my society will do."

But it gets much worse.

For in this same passage Berlin declares that what these absolute "rules or commandments" defining the sacredness of the liberal private sphere "will have in common" is, "that they are accepted so widely, and are grounded so deeply in the actual human nature of men as they have developed through history, as to be, by now, an essential part of what we mean by being a normal human being." And yet on the very next page (ibid., 51–52) Berlin is driven to grossly contradict himself: now he declares that "freedom from" and "freedom to" are "two profoundly divergent and irreconcilable attitudes to the ends of life," each of which "makes absolute claims," which "cannot both be fully satisfied," but each of whose "satisfaction" is "an ultimate value" that "*has an equal right to be classed among the deepest interests of mankind*" (my italics). Berlin desperately wants to defend liberal tolerance as a natural right, as an expression of what is "essential" to a "normal human"; but something strangely powerful possesses him to such a degree that he feels compelled to acknowledge the "equal right" (as an expression of "the deepest interests of humanity") of the *rejection* of liberal tolerance—in the name of its "irreconcilable" antagonist, "positive liberty."

THE SLIDE INTO LIBERAL OBSCURANTISM

Keeping this vivid example afforded by the self-contradictory incoherence of Isaiah Berlin before us, if we now return to Strauss's presentation, in the fourth paragraph of the Introduction to *Natural Right and History,* of the unfolding drama of liberal relativism, we find Strauss remarking that when, or insofar as, liberals have reacted to their recognition of this sort of contradiction (that we find illustrated in Berlin) by totally abandoning even the most minimal absolutes of natural right, and choosing "the uninhibited cultivation" of diversity and individuality, then "tolerance appeared as one value or ideal among many, and not intrinsically superior to its opposite." Since absolute, universal, and unchanging, "natural" standards have been abandoned, there are no rational grounds left for contending that the "values or ideals" entailing intolerance are not "equal in dignity to [those entailing] tolerance."

Indeed, there are no longer any rational grounds left for rejecting or choosing any ideal—tolerant or intolerant, humane or hateful: all ideals, as ideals, are equal in the eyes of reason; all have equal, or indeed the same, "grounds"—that is, the same absence of grounds. The only remaining basis for allegiance to any ideal is a groundless choice, or a groundless surrender to an ingrained preference for one's own fated tradition, culture, or civilization.

"But," Strauss continues, "it is practically impossible to leave it at the equality of all preferences or choices." If "the unequal rank of choices cannot be traced to the unequal rank of their objectives, it must be traced to the unequal rank of the acts of choosing"; and "this means eventually that genuine choice, as distinguished from spurious or despicable choice," is identified as "nothing but resolute or deadly serious decision" (this terminology evokes Heidegger). But such a decision "is akin to intolerance rather than to tolerance." The "liberal relativism" that is the outgrowth of the Lockean "natural right tradition of tolerance," or "the notion that everyone has a natural right to the pursuit of happiness as he understands happiness" becomes "a seminary of intolerance."

Thus we find even Isaiah Berlin, in the culmination of his argument, endorsing the following chilling and quasi-Heideggerian asseveration that he attributes to "an admirable writer [namely, Joseph Schumpeter] of our time" (Berlin, 1958, 57): "to realize the relative validity of one's convictions and yet stand for them unflinchingly, is what distinguishes a civilized man from a barbarian." [15] Strauss comments: "Berlin cannot escape the necessity to which every thinking being is subject: to take a final stand, an absolute stand." But what is this stand that Berlin winds up taking? It is this: only those relativists who are resolute or "unflinching" in their commitments (to whatever they may be committed, as relativists), are civilized; as for everybody else—for instance, the irresolute and hesitant or searching, or, on the other hand, the non-relativists who believe themselves to have discovered the truth—they are to be regarded as barbarians. As Strauss points out, this would imply that "every resolute liberal hack or thug would be a civilized man, while Plato and Kant would be barbarians."

Of course, Berlin, and those "generous liberals" who follow or adopt something like his position, never intend this conclusion that is necessarily entailed by their argument; all the more amazing and disconcerting is it that such intelligent and good-willed people wind up in such a dark and darkening corner.

Naturally, it is impossible for relativists to live with the nihilism into which their reasoning inevitably drags them. In the fifth or central paragraph of the introduction to *Natural Right and History,* Strauss reveals that nihilism is not, in fact, the truly ultimate *practical* outcome of relativism. For nihilism contradicts life and especially political life, because it contradicts moral responsibility and wholehearted loyalty to one's society: therefore nihilism is not humanly tenable in the long run. Yet nihilism is the logical outcome necessarily and irresistibly deduced by reason from relativism, and specifically from our liberal society's reigning commitment to unqualified respect for diversity or individuality. "The more we cultivate reason, the more we cultivate nihilism." So: since life itself rejects nihilism, "in order to live, we have to silence the easily silenced voice of reason." That is, "the inescapable practical consequence of nihilism is fanatical obscurantism," i.e., the desperately moralistic flight from reasoning—or from what reason reveals—about the apparent groundlessness of our moral and civic being. As Strauss put it in another study: "The result is visible in practically every curriculum and textbook of our time. One has the impression that the question of the nature of political things has been superseded by the question of the characteristic 'trends' of the social life of the present and of their historical origins, and that the question of the best, or the just, political order has been superseded by the question of the probable or desirable future" (WIPP, 59). Everything possible is done to hide from ourselves and our students the radical, genuinely liberating but necessarily frightening, questions about how we are to evaluate and judge our society as a whole and its historical trajectory.

THE DANGER LURKING IN THE REACTION
AGAINST LIBERAL RELATIVISM

In the sixth paragraph of the Introduction to *Natural Right and History,* Strauss adds the surprising and disturbing warning that precisely our indignant aversion to this outcome may "lead us to embrace natural right in a spirit of fanatical obscurantism." The embrace of natural right, without a full and certain rational proof of its validity—the embrace of natural right especially in a spirit of indignation against "the nihilists," or even against the "fanatical obscurantists"—could well be itself the expression of a fanatical obscurantism. Such an embrace could constitute nothing less than the betrayal or "destruction of reason"—and would be thus an implicit expression of, rather than an escape from, nihilism.[16]

Let us pause to observe that Strauss thus begins his most synoptic work with a very prominent warning against what might be called "Straussianism." This was by no means Strauss's sole such warning (see esp. Tarcov 1991). Yet Strauss also insisted that the problem of philosophic "sectarianism" was much more complex than is usually realized today. The history of classical philosophy, which did full justice to the fact that "the philosopher is as philosopher in need of friends" (since philo-sophy "is not wisdom but quest for wisdom"), proves that "philosophy, as distinguished from wisdom, *necessarily* appears in the form of philosophic schools or sects." Strauss emphatically agreed with his Hegelian opponent Alexandre Kojève's observation that "the danger cannot be avoided by abandoning the sect in favor of" the consensus generated by so-called respectable intellectual opinion, or what the French call the Republic of Letters. For "the first article of the constitution of the Republic of Letters stipulates that no philosophic persuasion must be taken too seriously." In other words, "a certain vague middle line, which is perhaps barely tolerable for the most easygoing members of the different persuasions if they are in their drowsiest mood, is set up as The Truth or as Common Sense; the substantive and irrepressible conflicts are dismissed as merely 'semantic.'" This means to say that "whereas the sect is narrow because it is passionately concerned with the true issues, the Republic of Letters is comprehensive because it is indifferent to the true issues." It follows that "if we have to choose between the sect and the Republic of Letters, we must choose the sect." But Strauss insists that this does not exhaust the options, for this does not yet do justice to the possible meaning of a philosophic "school" in the classic sense—

> Philosophy as such is nothing but genuine awareness of the problems, i.e., of the fundamental and comprehensive problems. It is impossible to think about these problems without becoming inclined toward a solution, toward one or another of the very few typical solutions. Yet as long as there is no wisdom but only quest for wisdom, the evidence of all solutions is necessarily smaller than the evidence of the problems. Therefore the philosopher ceases to be a philosopher at the moment at which his "subjective certainty" of a solution becomes stronger than his awareness of the problematic character of that solution. At that moment the sectarian is born. The danger of succumbing to the attraction of solutions is essential to philosophy which, without incurring this danger, would degenerate into playing with the problems. But the philosopher does not necessarily succumb to this danger, as is shown by Socrates, who never belonged to a sect and never founded one. And even [Strauss pregnantly and Delphically adds] if the philosophic friends are compelled to be members of a sect or to found one, they are not necessarily members of one and the same sect: *Amicus Plato*. (WIPP, 114–16)[17]

To return to the Introduction to *Natural Right and History:* in the next or seventh paragraph Strauss deepens his admonition by cautioning that the uncovering of the genealogy of the idea of natural right will, "contrary to a popular notion," "aggravate rather than remove the difficulty of an impartial treatment"—or of what Strauss characterized in the previous paragraph as the needed "cautious," "detached, theoretical, impartial discussion" of the "problem of natural right" (NRH, pp. 6–7).

Strauss is certainly at pains to remind the reader whose strong uneasiness and hopes he is arousing that that anxiety and those hopes seek something that transcends even patriotism: the "need for natural right," the need that is "as evident today as it has been for centuries and even millennia," includes the human need for liberation from spiritual slavery to the ideal of our own society; "the mere fact that we can raise the question of the worth of the ideal of our society shows that there is something in man that is not altogether in slavery to his society, and therefore that we are able, and hence obliged, to look for a standard with reference to which we can judge of the ideals of our own as well as of any other society" (NRH, para. 2, p. 3).

STRAUSS'S TROUBLING QUESTIONS

The first seven paragraphs of the Introduction to *Natural Right and History* thus quietly but insistently pose, for the attentive and questing reader, the following cascade of disquieting questions. To what extent is the historical outcome, in our time, of the specifically modern natural rights doctrine that inspires and finds expression in the Declaration of Independence necessary, or inevitable—thereby revealing a lack of solid grounds for that doctrine from its inception? Or, alternatively, to what extent is this historical development an unfortunate accident, or series of forgetful mistakes—from which we might recover, by retrieving the pristine original, by reelaborating the cogency of the rigorous and comprehensive argumentation from truly "self-evident" premises that proves conclusively the truth of the Lockean natural rights doctrine? What is the decisive series of forgetful mistakes, or what are the unanswered (unanswerable?) needs, that in the course of modern history has eventually rendered the Lockean doctrine of natural right—of the natural (universal and fixed) rights to life, liberty, and the pursuit of happiness—unsustainable, and, what is worse, ultimately productive of nihilism, or of fanatical obscurantism, and hence of the abandonment of reason or of rationalism altogether?

Most specifically, why are the contemporary progeny of Locke, "the generous liberals," impelled, out of some kind of awe or shame before "diversity or individuality," to disown their belief in the rationally knowable, unchanging, and universal goodness or rightness even of tolerance? What power radiates from diversity or individuality, to shake so profoundly the late-modern West, driving generous liberals to conceive of their tolerance merely as an "ideal" of our own particular historical culture or civilization? What is the allure of diversity and individuality that makes the late-modern heirs to the "faith" in Lockean natural rights forsake that faith, to "welcome with relief" the "yoke" of "German thought," consisting in the imposition of historical relativism? And why is it all too likely that even or precisely the renewed embrace of natural right, in re-action, will itself be an expression of fanatic fear—rather than love or acceptance—of the truth disclosed by reason? Precisely what is it about this truth, about *the* truth, that makes it so profoundly disconcerting? Is it really the truth that is bad or ugly? Or is the problem at bottom our unhealthy reaction to the truth, a reaction due to some terrible weakness or confusion of ours—either historically acquired (and hence, we might hope, perhaps historically curable), or lamentably intrinsic to the human condition? If the last, is the weakness or confusion inescapable by all—or is it only ubiquitous among us?

PLUMBING THE DEPTHS OF THE CRISIS

It is now obvious that Strauss does not understand our crisis, this crisis of our universal "culture" of normative reason or science, to be caused by moral lapses or weaknesses of character—by our loss of will, or by our self-indulgent permissiveness, or by our failure of fidelity to our "Great Tradition." In Strauss's diagnosis, these are all symptoms or effects, not causes. The causes lie deep within the problematic character of our Great Tradition.

Our Great Tradition as it is handed down to us is riven, Strauss contends, by two throbbing tensions that have been often and in many ways buried, masked, or denied but have never been resolved. These discords Strauss terms (borrowing from illustrious predecessors) "the Quarrel Between the Ancients and the Moderns," and (with a bow to Spinoza's felicitous formulation) "the theologico-political problem"—meaning, more expansively, "the conflict between the Biblical and the philosophic notions of the good life."

"The quarrel between the ancients and the moderns" is the term some of the great protagonists gave to the vast philosophic, scientific, political, and cultural struggle that took place in Europe in the sixteenth and seventeenth centuries, when the previously reigning authority of classical rationalism (above all Aristotle) was overthrown and replaced with a new, antagonistic modern rationalism—whose eventual historical development has culminated in our crisis.

"The theologico-political problem" Strauss articulates, in a nutshell, as the "fundamental question," whether "men can acquire that knowledge of the good without which they cannot guide their lives individually or collectively by the unaided efforts of their natural powers, or whether they are dependent for that knowledge on Divine Revelation." "No alternative," Strauss continues, "is more fundamental than this: . . . a life of obedient love versus a life of free insight." And, he adds, "In every attempt at harmonization, in every synthesis however impressive, one of the two opposed elements is sacrificed, more or less subtly but in any event surely, to the other" (NRH, 74–75). The fundamental problem of human existence is a theologico-*political,* and not merely a theological problem because its most important meaning and bearing is not only theological but political: at stake is the ultimate source of our norms of justice or righteousness, the norms by which we guide our lives as citizens, ultimately citizens of the world, obligated to one another, and not merely concerned with and for our poor individual selves.

The contested alternative that is the theologico-political problem is more fundamental than the contested alternative "ancients versus moderns." For at the heart of the quarrel between the ancients and the moderns Strauss finds a quarrel over the proper philosophic response to the theologico-political problem. Ever since the dawn of the modern Enlightenment, the West has been in large part captivated or dominated by an increasingly desperate attempt to assert and to believe that the theologico-political problem—the tension that is at the very heart of the West, the tension between "Jerusalem and Athens"—has been or can be adequately disposed of, if not overcome, in a way and to a degree undreamed of by the ancient philosophers and their medieval heirs. I believe Strauss understands the crisis of our times to represent nothing less than the eruption into broad daylight of the ultimate and complex historical consequences of the modern West's long incubating self-doubts in this crucial regard.

This means to say that Strauss understands "the crisis of our times" as "the crisis of the West." Ours is a crisis that exposes the untenability of the Western tradition in its historically developed, present form. Truly to understand the gravity of the crisis of our times is to see the absurdity of trying simply to reinvigorate, and to rededicate ourselves to continuing, our Western tradition, as it has been given to us. The Western tradition as it has nurtured and shaped us has become bewildered and bewildering. But we cannot simply jettison what the West has become or has made us into; we cannot magically reconstitute ourselves or try to leap out of history. Neither can we leap back, over this history, to some earlier epoch, be it medieval or ancient, or early modern. For the early "moderns" were not without impressive grounds for their acute dissatisfaction with the "ancient" (and the medieval) responses to the theologico-political problem; and the later moderns were not without impressive grounds for their acute dissatisfaction with their earlier modern predecessors. We cannot simply return to the ancients: we have to reopen the quarrel between the ancients and the moderns. We have to retrieve, to rethink, to relive that quarrel, at its deepest philosophic level, in its unfolding complexity, and without any *parti pris*.

Gripped by the crisis of our times, we have to launch a strenuous struggle for self-critical understanding of what has become of the West and why—in a search for the possibility of salvaging what can and should be salvaged, as the core of a genuinely reasonable life, based on and resigned to the knowable limits of our powers. We can take heart from the paradoxical and initially mysterious watchword of all authentic Socratic rationalism: *human wisdom is knowledge of ignorance*. As Strauss explains, "Knowledge of ignorance is not ignorance. It is knowledge of the elusive character of the truth, of the whole. Socrates, then, viewed man in the light of the mysterious character of the whole. He held therefore that we are more familiar with the situation of man as man than with the ultimate causes of that situation. We may also say that he viewed man in the light of the unchangeable ideas, i.e., of the fundamental and permanent problems."

This last sentence begins to take us into Strauss's highly controversial interpretation of the true, hidden, and lost meaning of the famous and apparently dogmatic-metaphysical Platonic "doctrine of ideas." On the basis of his controversial new interpretation of the Platonic dialogues, Strauss utterly rejects today's universal scholarly assumption that Plato was a "Platonist." Before we launch into even a preliminary introduction to Strauss's revolutionary Plato reinterpretation (and its critical importance for our world), we need to listen to the cautionary admonitions Strauss issues at the outset of the voyage he invites us to undertake with him.

For Strauss emphatically warns that our journey cannot have any successful outcome if we fall prey to the natural temptation to insist that we must, come what may, return with the answers for which we seek. One "is not likely to return to the shores of our time as exactly the same man who departed from them" (NIPPP, 331). In the course of the voyage, Strauss predicts, our very questions may well undergo a metamorphosis. Whatever answers we find, if they are to be true and not merely another set of temporarily comforting illusions or excuses for thinking, must be answers that arise from the truth of the matters that we discover and not from our passionate wishes. Our discoveries must chastise our wishes. We cannot be sure that the crisis that propels us into this struggle is a crisis capable of being surmounted. We may finally discover the truth of what the singularly intransigent as well as profound thinker of this crisis, Heidegger, calls the angst-ridden uncovering of "the nothing" or *nihil* into which and out of which all humans are "thrown" by Destiny or Being—and about which we as humans in this epoch are given the dubious privilege of becoming self-conscious. Strauss offers no certainty and no promise in this regard (NRH, 6–7). What he offers is no more and no less than this: a path, the sole path, that can be taken by anyone who, as a necessary consequence of seriously facing our predicament, in honesty or intellectual probity as well as prudence, has no choice but to seek to overcome this crisis—or to understand that and why it cannot be overcome.

To avoid misunderstandings, it is essential to add at once that Strauss does not suppose that the most profound contradiction at the heart of the Great Tradition of the West—the conflict between philosophic reason (or science), and prophetic scriptural revelation—in and of itself renders the Western tradition untenable, or even weak. On the contrary. The key perennial practical as well as theoretical challenge the West has always faced is, how and whether the custodians of the Great Tradition, in each epoch, keep alive this titanic controversy. We too in our time are called to this task, although the reigning relativism that is our dying version of the Western tradition tries to deny this challenge and this call. In Strauss's words, "it seems to me that this antagonism must be considered by us in action." As he proceeds to make clear, the "action" he has in mind is argumentation, rigorous dialogue: that is to say, "the core, the nerve, of Western intellectual history, Western spiritual history, one could almost say, is the conflict between the Biblical and the philosophic notions of the good life," which has "showed itself primarily, of course, in arguments—arguments advanced by theologians on behalf of the Biblical point of view and by philosophers on behalf of the philosophic point of view." On this level of argumentation, "it seems to me that this unresolved conflict is the secret of the vitality of Western civilization. The recognition of two conflicting roots of Western civilization is, at first, a very disconcerting observation. Yet this realization has also something reassuring and comforting about it. The very life of Western civilization is the life between two codes, a fundamental tension. There is therefore no reason inherent in Western civilization itself, in its fundamental constitution, why it should give up life. But this comforting thought is justified only if we live that life, if we live that conflict" (RCPR, 270).

In the opening of a chapter he contributed to an undergraduate textbook that he edited, Strauss gives a more specific indication of what it means to "live that conflict"; he does so by providing a pointer to the thinkers and the texts that should initially spur and guide the argumentation:

Men often speak of virtue without using the word but saying instead "the quality of life" or "the great society" or "ethical" or even "square." But do we know what virtue is? Socrates arrived at the conclusion that it is the greatest good for a human being to make everyday speeches about virtue—apparently without ever finding a completely satisfactory definition of it. However, if we seek the most elaborate and least ambiguous answer to this truly vital question, we shall turn to Aristotle's *Ethics*. There we read among other things that there is a virtue of the first order called magnanimity—the habit of claiming high honors for oneself with the understanding that one is worthy of them. We also read there that sense of shame is not a virtue: sense of shame is becoming for the young who, due to their immaturity, cannot help making mistakes, but not for mature and well-bred men who simply always do the right and proper thing. Wonderful as all this is—we have received a very different message from a very different quarter. When the prophet Isaiah received his vocation, he was overpowered by the sense of his unworthiness: "I am a man of unclean lips amidst a people of unclean lips." This amounts to an implicit condemnation of magnanimity and an explicit vindication of the sense of shame. The reason is given in the context: "holy, holy, holy is the lord of hosts." There is no holy god for Aristotle and the Greeks generally. Who is right, the Greeks or the Jews? Athens or Jerusalem? And how to proceed in order to find out who is right? Must we not admit that human wisdom is unable to settle this question and that every answer is based on an act of faith? But does this not constitute the complete and final defeat of Athens? For a philosophy based on faith is no longer philosophy. Perhaps it was this unresolved conflict which has prevented Western thought from ever coming to rest. Perhaps it is this conflict which is at the bottom of a kind of thought which is philosophic indeed but no longer Greek: modern philosophy. It is in trying to understand modern philosophy that we come across Machiavelli. (HPP, 296–97)

The quest that Strauss thus adumbrates is a Socratic quest or *skepsis* (though it is of course a late-modern quest, and thus not a quest that Socrates himself was ever required or enabled to undertake). In order to consider whether to follow Strauss in this search or *zetesis,* it is of the utmost importance that we try to begin to understand better the chasm that separates nonabsolutist "zetetic skepticism" (as Strauss terms it) from the relativism that is the core of our crisis.

SOCRATIC ZETETIC SKEPTICISM VERSUS LATE-MODERN RELATIVISM

Relativism comes in a range of forms. At a lower reach of the range there is the more common, less thoughtful type: the relativism that views all ultimate "values" as radically subjective and hence equal. The practical consequence of this more vulgar variant is a shallow nihilism that is unlivable and that therefore always in one way or another becomes self-contradictory and fanatically obscurantist. But there is a far more sophisticated and sternly intransigent type of relativism, growing out of the German idealist tradition and reaching its culmination in Nietzsche's thought, radicalized by Heidegger. This relativism looks down with contempt not only on scientific positivism, but on liberalism and on the individualistic and egalitarian expressions of relativism. Strauss circumscribes as follows the core of this deeper and more grimly challenging relativism.

In response to contemporary science's claim to deal with "facts," and thus to find an island of nonevaluating objectivity that is insulated from contaminating determination by "subjective values," historicism counters that "every understanding, however theoretical, implies specific evaluations." For science is "said to be a body of true propositions." But these propositions are all "answers to questions." What a valid *answer* consists of "may be determined by the rules or principles of logic"; "but the *questions* depend on one's direction of interest, and hence on one's values," which are "subjective" or, more adequately expressed, are "dependent on the society" to which and in which the science and its human practitioners belong (WIPP, 25–26).

For "values" are not purely individual creations or choices, the radical historicist insists. They are rather choices and creations of individuals living within and shaped by diverse, conflicting, and ever mutating specific historical-cultural matrices. More than that. "Values," the radical historicist contends, are a manifestation of radically temporal and contingent "life" or "existence" — whose universal contours can, to some limited but crucial extent, be grasped, in varying degrees in various epochs and cultural "horizons." Our epoch is one that is paradoxically privileged in this regard. Ours is the disillusioned epoch, the epoch of the decisive insight and hence the greatest danger but also the greatest promise. In recognizing this, one sees that all "values" are far from being equal in dignity, and that the claim that values are equal in dignity is merely the expression of a peculiarly impoverished or lifeless and hence inferior horizon. The equalization of values is the greatest danger. Values and cultures can and must be ranked in accordance with the degree of resoluteness or seriousness with which the basic values are held or advanced, and in accordance with their depth or shallowness, their comprehensiveness or narrowness, their honesty or hypocrisy, their communal responsibility or irresponsibility, their degree of veneration for their past and of revolutionary creativity looking to their future.

Yet none of these and kindred criteria, one by one or all together, constitute an adequate account of what is humanly good, high, or right — or bad, low, or wrong. Criteria such as those just mentioned, the radical historicist insists, allow no more than a kind of formal and preliminary ranking. None of these criteria allow us to speak of human "nature" in more than a very loose sense. There is not "the" good society, or "the" human condition, or even "the" (permanent) human problems or alternatives. The general or universal characteristics of "values" and of the problems they pose for living humans always require completion through unique and essentially temporal or impermanent specification. (For example, one can speak of the necessity for "family values" in any healthy culture, and one can even specify certain essential features of family values, such as respect for parents and the nurturing of children, etc.; but these family values must be made much, much more specific to attain their concrete meaning — because the human family, as is obvious from the least survey of rich and profound historical cultures, is distinguished by incalculably diverse and antagonistic forms of matriarchy or patriarchy, of monogamy or polygamy, of linkage to monotheisms or to polytheisms, of postures toward homosexuality, etc., etc.)

"The crucial issue," Strauss writes in summarizing this "thoughtful historicist" position (WIPP, 26–27), "concerns the status of those permanent characteristics of humanity, such as the distinction between the noble and the base, which are admitted by the thoughtful historicists: can these permanencies be used as criteria for distinguishing between good and bad dispensations of fate? The historicist answers this question in the negative. He looks down on the permanencies in question because of their objective, common, superficial and rudimentary character: to become relevant, they would have to be completed, and their completion is no longer common but historical." The grim political implication becomes clear when Strauss adds: "It was the contempt for these permanencies which permitted the most radical historicist in 1933 to submit to, or rather to welcome, as a dispensation of fate, the verdict of the least wise and least moderate part of his nation while it was in its least wise and least moderate mood, and at the same time to speak of wisdom and moderation."

Over and against "the historicist contention" stands the Socratic self-vindication, as Strauss resurrects it (NRH, 32, 35–36). Historicism, Strauss charges, not only fails to prove, it does not really even *argue* for the validity of the unprecedented, late-modern "experience of history" (that is, the purported "experience" of the historical mutability of *all* human thought). "In the transition from early (theoretical) to radical ('existentialist') historicism, the 'experience of history' was never submitted to critical analysis." Instead, "it was taken for granted" that this "is a genuine experience and not a questionable interpretation of experience." The question was not even raised, "whether what is really experienced does not allow of an entirely different and possibly more adequate interpretation"—the indication of which interpretation is perhaps the deepest intention of Strauss in *Natural Right and History* (not to mention all his other writings on modernity, and his discovery of esoteric writing). Above all, the definitive "experience of history" does not, Strauss insists, "make doubtful the view that the fundamental problems, such as the problems of justice, persist or retain their identity in all historical change, however much they may be obscured by the temporary denial of their relevance and however variable or provisional all human solutions to these problems may be." "No more is needed," Strauss continues, "to legitimate philosophy in its original, Socratic sense": "philosophy in the full sense of the term" is "possible" if, and "only if man, while incapable of acquiring wisdom or full understanding of the whole, is capable of knowing what he does not know, that is to say, of grasping the fundamental problems"—and, therewith, "the fundamental alternatives regarding their solution," which "are, in principle, coeval with human thought."

Yet here we encounter one of the most enigmatic aspects of Strauss's self-definition as a Socratic. For Strauss goes on to acknowledge that "if political philosophy is limited to understanding the fundamental alternative [sing.], it is of no practical value." It would be "unable to answer the question of what the ultimate goal of wise action is." It would "have to delegate the crucial decision to blind choice." Now, Strauss observes, "the whole galaxy of political philosophers from Plato to Hegel, and certainly all adherents of natural right, assumed that the fundamental political problem is susceptible of a final solution." Strauss obviously provokes the question (which would of course be asked at once by his historicist dialectical interlocutor): what if anything is the ground for this momentous "assumption" that pervades and characterizes all genuine political philosophy?

Strauss answers: "this assumption ultimately rested on the Socratic answer to the question of how man ought to live." And what is that answer? Strauss replies: "by realizing that we are ignorant of the most important things, we realize at the same time that the most important thing for us, or the one thing needful, is quest for knowledge of the most important things or quest for wisdom." But how does this answer amount to a "final solution" to "the fundamental political problem"? Strauss shows that he is acutely aware of, and even means to provoke in the reader, this question, as he cryptically replies: "that this conclusion is not barren of political consequences is known to every reader of Plato's *Republic* or of Aristotle's *Politics*." Now what does this remark mean? While "every reader" of these works can recognize that they are "not barren" of political consequences, it is hardly the case that every reader discerns, in either or both of the works to which Strauss here refers, the final solution to the fundamental political problem. Moreover, even some rather competent readers (e.g., Hegel), who seem to have found in Plato's *Republic* and Aristotle's *Politics* a cornerstone of what they understood to be the complete solution, seem to have disagreed deeply with Aristotle and with Plato (or his Socrates) as to the character of that solution.

But did even those rather competent readers have the requisite patience and docility to figure out the political consequences that Plato and Aristotle intended to teach? Did they take seriously enough the pervasiveness of Platonic and Socratic irony? Or were they among the "many interpreters of Plato" who "do not sufficiently consider the possibility that his Socrates was as much concerned with understanding what justice is, i.e., with understanding the whole complexity of the problem of justice, as with preaching justice?" For "if one is concerned with understanding the problem of justice, one must go through the stage in which justice presents itself as identical with citizen-morality, and one must not merely rush through that stage"—a "stage" that Strauss identifies as depicted above all by Socrates' conversation with Polemarchus in Book One of the *Republic*. That conversation, Strauss indicates, must be estimated and studied in light of the passage in the *Phaedrus* that informs us that Polemarchus is one of the very few characters in the Platonic dialogues who in Socrates' opinion made the transition from citizen youth to philosophic youth (NRH, 150n).

This much is indisputable: Strauss could not have made it clearer that our coming to understand what he means by the "Socratic answer" depends on our following with care and then imitating on our own Strauss's detailed interpretations of Plato's *Republic* and Aristotle's *Politics*—as well as his interpretations of the great medievals, the Jew Maimonides, the Muslim al-Fārābī, and the Christian Marsilius, each of whom upheld the adequacy of the classical "solution" in the face and context of the revealed religions of Scripture. Those interpretations are provided, however, only in part by Strauss's essays devoted to those works; those essays must be supplemented by the ubiquitous reference to Plato and Aristotle that pervades all Strauss's other works; they must be supplemented, above all, by Strauss's extensive and detailed interpretations of the Socratic writings of Xenophon. But this only means to say that Strauss's interpretations that answer or resolve the puzzle we have identified are in largest part available only to the readers who put together for themselves Strauss's didactically subtle interpretations.[18]

The grave puzzle that we are now focusing upon intensifies as Strauss goes on to concede that "the perennial conflict between the Socratic and the anti-Socratic answer" (to the question how man ought to live) "creates the impression that the Socratic answer is as arbitrary as its opposite, or that the perennial conflict is insoluble." Those who are under the spell of this impression are led to the un-Socratic but also unhistoricist position that Strauss finds expressed at the most serious level of Max Weber's thinking, which is representative of a scientific relativism that transcends vulgar relativism and, in at least one—or even the crucial—respect, stands closer to Strauss and to Socratism than anything found in Heidegger or radical historicism.

Strauss confronts Max Weber as an impressive representative of all those "who are not historicists," because they "do admit the existence of fundamental and unchanging alternatives," but nevertheless "deny that human reason is capable of solving the conflict between these alternatives." For Weber, "the ultimate values are as timeless as the principles of logic"; and "it is the recognition of timeless values that distinguishes Weber's position most significantly from historicism" (NRH, 36 and 39). But why, according to Strauss, was Weber impelled to the un-Socratic conclusion that "the conflict between ultimate values cannot be resolved by human reason" (ibid., 64)? Strauss gives the following answer (ibid., 72–74).

Weber agreed with Socrates that "science or philosophy" is "the way toward freedom from delusion; it is the foundation of a free life, of a life that refuses to bring the sacrifice of the intellect and dares to look reality in its stern face." But Weber identified "science or philosophy" with contemporary, late-modern science or philosophy—in itself and in its manifest consequences for the whole of our contemporary historical existence. Weber saw that "the thought of the present age is characterized by disenchantment or unqualified 'this-worldliness,' or irreligion"; "but he was certain that all devotion to causes or ideals has its roots in religious faith and, therefore, that the decline of religious faith will ultimately lead to the extinction of all causes or ideals." He "despaired of the modern this-worldly irreligious experiment, and yet he remained attached to it because he was fated to believe in science as he understood it." And "the result of this conflict, which he could not resolve, was his belief that the conflict of values cannot be resolved by human reason."[19]

In other words: Weber shares with historicism the false assumption that reason as it expresses itself in today's science and philosophy is the perfection of reason and "the perfection of man's natural understanding of the natural world." He and all our contemporaries fail to appreciate fully the degree to which modern reason is historically and thus epistemologically derivative. They fail to recognize the degree to which, in the course of the derivation, an absolutely crucial foundation has been buried and lost. Our science and philosophy are the products of a four-centuries-old tradition that has more or less deliberately sought to transform existence and thus has covered over the truly natural human world and consciousness. The late-modern "scientific understanding of the world emerges by way of a radical modification, as distinguished from a perfection, of the natural understanding." Modern science and philosophy have lost sight of what is required to establish the ground of science or philosophy, through a lucid and continuous ascent from the "pre-scientific" world—"the world in which we live," the world of "common-sense" (NRH, 79). Yet the genuine "common-sense" world is of far less easy access than is generally recognized.

The "natural world" is "the world in which we live and act." It is thus "not the object or the product of a theoretical attitude; it is a world not of mere objects at which we detachedly look but of 'things' or 'affairs' which we handle." But: "as long as we identify the natural or pre-scientific world with the world in which we live, we are dealing with an abstraction." For "the world in which we live is already a product of science, or at any rate it is profoundly affected by the existence of science." In order "to grasp the natural world as a world that is radically pre-scientific or pre-philosophic, one has to go back behind the first emergence of science or philosophy." One of course cannot do this through "anthropology," for that is to impose immediately the interpretive categories of the science of anthropology—i.e., of modern science or of modern philosophy—on the phenomena; and it is precisely those modern categories that are in question. The only satisfactorily liberated access to the natural world that we possess is through the texts of classical philosophy supplemented by the scriptures. "The information that classical philosophy supplies about its origins suffices, especially if that information is supplemented by consideration of the most elementary premises of the Bible" (NRH, 79–80).

For it is no exaggeration to say that the chief and pervasive intention of the Platonic and Xenophontic Socrates' political philosophizing, as disclosed by Strauss's interpretations, is to preserve, in order to show the evident necessity of the ascent from, the pre-scientific world, including above all "the most elementary premises of the Bible" (premises that are not of course the theme of the Bible). Historicism as well as the Weberian belief in the irresolvable conflict of timeless ultimate values "may blur, but they cannot extinguish, the evidence of those simple experiences regarding right and wrong which are at the bottom of the philosophic contention that there is a natural right" (NRH, 31–32). The painstaking clarification of what is implied in these "most elementary experiences," as they are expressed in the opinions of thoughtful and experienced people who are prephilosophic and prescientific, is the core of the Socratic way to the solution—by way of a "philosophy of the human things," i.e., "the just and noble things."

This carries an important and controversial implication, which defines one of the most distinctive features of Strauss's understanding of classical political philosophy as Socratic political philosophy.[20] Strauss denies that the primary theme of classical political philosophy is human nature, let alone that classical political philosophy begins from specific assumptions about human nature. Classical philosophy moves to, or issues in, an account of human nature, but it begins from and is based, even centered, on a conversational questioning of authoritative and widespread or universal moral opinion (common sense): "human nature is one thing, virtue or the perfection of human nature is another. The definite character of the virtues and, in particular, of justice cannot be deduced from human nature"; "virtue exists in most cases, if not in all cases," in "speech rather than in deed." "Plato does not," in other words, "oppose to materialist-mechanistic physics a spiritualist-teleological physics (*Phaedo* 100c-e), but keeps to what can be understood without any far-fetched 'tragic' apparatus, to what the 'Athenians' *say* (cf. *Meno,* 75b-d with 76d-e; cf. further, *Phaedo,* 100c-e)." But "what men say" is "*contradictory.*" The "contradictions make necessary an investigation into which of the conflicting assertions is true." The result is, that "one of the conflicting *endoxa* ["common sense" opinions] must be given up, the opposed *endoxon* must be maintained." Thus the latter ceases to be simply common sense, and becomes "truly paradoxical": "*but by making unanimity and understanding of each with himself and with others possible, it proves itself true* (cf. *Republic,* 457b and *Crito,* 46d-e) [my italics]."[21] And "the art of the truth-revealing discussion [*mit-einander-sprechen*], *of dialectic,* is nothing else but directing the discussion in the right way and at the right time to the true *endoxon* which is to be maintained."

Now "the most obvious contradictions which underlie every contention and every enmity, concern the just, the beautiful, and the good (*Euthyphro* 7b-d, and *Phaedrus* 263a; cf. *Republic* 523a-524c)"; and "yet men are in greater accord as regards the good than as regards any other subject, and in such a fashion that *this real concord is the ultimate ground of all possible concord* [my italics]."[22] For "all *say* of the good that they really wish it." And "that means that they want the truly good [das Gute *selbst*] and not merely the *appearance* of good (*Republic,* 505d-e and *Theaetetus,* 177d; cf. Aristotle's *Rhetoric,* i, 7, #36-37; cf. *Theaetetus,* 167; *Euthy-*

demus, 286bff., and *Cratylus,* 385eff.)" — "and further that they *wish* to have it, to possess it; they pursue it, they desire it, they know, therefore, that they *lack* it (*Symposium* 204a and 204e-205d; cf. *Meno* 77c–d, *Gorgias,* 468d, *Euthydemus,* 278e-280b, *Hippias Major,* 291c–d and 294a)." Only "a moment's reflection shows that what men usually conceive of as good—wealth, honours, and so forth— is not the same good as they *mean;* for they mean by 'good' what is in every respect the contrary of evil, that which is completely free from evil." But "men also say: that the good is virtue and wisdom/ insight [*Einsicht*]"; and "it is precisely of this better understood good that what men say of misunderstood good holds: that only by partaking of the true external *transcendent* good as such, which is the ground of their virtue and wisdom/insight, are men virtuous and wise/insightful [*einsichtig*]."[23] Such "true virtue" differs from "pseudo-virtue" or "apparent virtue [*Scheintugend*]"[24] in this, "that true virtue has as its basis a complete change of objective or orientation [*Blickrichtung*]," whereas apparent virtue "is based entirely on ordinary human aims and interests." True virtue as opposed to apparent virtue "is the result of 'divinely inspired madness,' a 'purification' of the soul, a conversion of the *whole* soul. It is essentially wisdom/insight (*Phaedo,* 68c-69c; *Phaedrus,* 244d and 256e; *Symposium,* 203a; cf. *Republic,* 518c and 521c)."

"One gains the clearest conception of the antithesis," between true and apparent or pseudovirtue, "if one compares the life and fate of a truly just man, who has no appearance of justice, whose justice is *hidden,* with the life and fate of a truly unjust man, who enjoys a reputation for justice and whose injustice is hidden (*Republic,* 365aff.)." For "Socrates-Plato," it is crucial that one "compares the just and the unjust, and not the *courageous* man and his opposite," even or precisely because "no virtue seems more brilliant (*N. Ethics,* 1177b16ff.), more worthy of reverence, than courage." And "yet it is the lowest virtue (*Laws,* 630c-631c; cf. 963eff.)." As such, it is the virtue that least reveals the heart of the matter. The reason comes to sight when one scrutinizes courage "not in its archaic form, in which its sense is, as it were, narrowed and limited by obedience to law (cf. *Protagoras,* 342b, with *Republic,* 429c-430c)," but rather "apart from this limitation, in itself." Then we see that "courage, as it is usually understood, is the virtue of the *man,* his capacity, without fear or effeminacy, to help himself, to protect himself from injustice or injury, to assert and save himself." But "according to this ideal, the perfect man is the *tyrant (Meno,* 71e; *Gorgias,* 469c, 483a–b, 491b, 512d; *Republic,* 549d-550a)," who is "the most seductive and therefore the most revealing form of the popular ideal of courage"—"and thus challenges to searching criticism of that ideal." This "ideal" is "nothing more noble, and nothing else, than a disguise of man's natural self-love, of man's natural hedonism (cf. *Protagoras,* 349d, with 351bff. as well as *Gorgias,* 492cff.)." Therefore "it is not courage which is the highest virtue— self-mastery stands higher, and higher still than self-mastery stand wisdom/insight, and justice."

The result of the sustained and soul-purifying critical meditation on justice, in relation to insight or wisdom, Strauss states as follows. "In itself wisdom stands supreme," but "for humans, justice [*für den Menschen jedoch die Gerechtigkeit*]": "however much the philosophers, assimilating themselves to God, transcend human limitations, they are, and remain, men, and thus form only one species of men among others, and are thus under allegiance to the *laws* of the State, which has as its aim the maintenance of the whole and not the happiness of the parts." The "law of the ideal State *compels* the philosophers to take thought for other men and to watch over them and not 'to turn whither each will' (*Republic,* 519d-520c)."

Yet at the start, certainly, and especially when we have not yet ourselves begun to taste and fully to experience the soul-transforming effects of the Socratic dialogue, properly understood, we must regard the entire attempt to recapture this true Socratic "solution" as tentative and experimental. Prior to the full "reconsideration of the most elementary premises of philosophy," Strauss stresses, "the issue of natural right can only remain an open question" (NRH, 31).

2 : The Revival of Classical Political Philosophy

In the massive foreground of Strauss's lifework stands his resuscitation of classical republican political theory, understood as emanating from the intellectual revolution effected in and by Socratic political philosophy. It is here that Strauss finds the standpoint for a searching and critical, while sympathetic and admiring, appraisal of our contemporary liberal democracy. It is here that Strauss finds the key to a recovery of our lost or obscured self-consciousness as moderns. For our civic existence is rooted in a vast cultural revolution—what was called the Enlightenment, of the seventeenth and eighteenth centuries— that defined itself in opposition to the previously regnant tradition that took its inspiration ultimately from the citizen-philosopher Socrates.

It follows that even or precisely if we wish passionately to reaffirm as true the modern principles of the Enlightenment, we are impelled to a fresh and unbiased immersion in classical political philosophy. For our modern principles are in question, or have become questionable; we are forced to try to defend them. But a "mere defense" is inadequate: one cannot merely be defensive about principles of right "without exposing oneself to the reasonable suspicion that one is defending a vested interest of some kind or other which does not bear being looked into by an impartial third." What is more, the mere resolution to defend one's principles or commitments "is particularly unbecoming for the adherents of the modern principles—principles that are inseparable from the demand for the liberation of one's mind from all prejudices." Indeed, "the very resolution to defend a position may be said to entail the loss of a most important freedom, a freedom the exercise of which was responsible for the success of the modern venture: defenders cannot afford radically to doubt." Thus, "the only answer to the attack on the modern principles which is legitimate on the basis of those principles themselves is their free and impartial reexamination." Now "the method of such reexamination is predetermined by the nature of the modern principles." For "they were evolved in opposition to, and by way of transformation of, the principles of classical philosophy." To such a degree is this true, that "up to the present day no adherent of the modern principles has been able to assert them with any degree of definiteness without explicitly and more or less passionately attacking the classical principles." It follows that "a free examination of the modern principles is necessarily based on their conscientious confrontation with those of classical philosophy."[1]

But the word "conscientious" in this context bears heavy freight. "The modern students of classical philosophy are modern men," formed entirely by modern principles. They "almost inevitably approach classical philosophy from a modern point of view." "Only if the study of classical philosophy were accompanied by constant and relentless reflection on the modern principles, and hence by liberation from the naive acceptance of those principles, could there be any prospect of an adequate understanding of classical philosophy by modern men."

This means to say that one must conduct one's study of classical philosophy by genuinely opening oneself to "the possibility that its teachings are simply true, or that it is decisively superior to modern philosophy." One must try to avoid the imposition of all modern categories and terminology. The student must "cease to take his bearings by the modern signposts with which he has grown familiar since his early childhood." Instead, "one must learn to take his bearings by the signposts that guided the classical philosophers." But these latter signposts "are not immediately visible," since they are buried from our sight under contemporary scholarship, and the modern or late-modern tradition from which that scholarship springs, which has imposed on the texts a thick blanket of modern, alien interpretations.[2]

The preceding "methodological" admonitions, written by Strauss when he first launched his project of reviving classical political philosophy, alert us to a salient characteristic of all Strauss's studies that has caused deleterious misunderstandings, especially among those who dabble in Strauss seeking evidence that might allow them to foist upon him one or another dogma (the dabblers I have in mind are chiefly the watchdog censors of the academic and intellectual establishment, but include even some among his defenders or disciples). Each of Strauss's major interpretive writings do exhibit him as a kind of disciple of the thinker that he is interpreting. Strauss never studies seriously a great thinker without trying in some measure to give himself provisionally but in earnest to that thinker. And this characteristic of Strauss's writings makes it easy for those who are seeking facile answers to the question of what Strauss stood for to find apparent evidence that he agreed with and took his bearings by one or another of the diverse and conflicting thinkers about whom he has written. Strauss can indeed be quoted to show that he was a disciple of Machiavelli, or of Nietzsche, or of Hobbes—or of al-Fārābī, of Maimonides, of Marsilius, of Rousseau, of Montesquieu, of Lessing—as well as of Socrates, Plato, or Aristotle. As regards each of the great thinkers whom he seriously studies, Strauss disciplines himself to see and even to feel the world through that thinker's eyes and sensibilities, to use only that thinker's categories and terminology, to show the force of that thinker's explicit or implicit critique of other competing views—in short, to find that thinker in his strength, while scorning to score points by highlighting tertiary weaknesses or failings.

Strauss in effect seriously experiments with (and tries to seduce his readers to follow him in experimenting with) becoming a convert, if you will, to each great thinker's argumentative power and revelatory insight into the phenomena. Strauss tries self-consciously to grasp and to show as fully and sympathetically as possible what it would mean to become a genuine "Aristotelian," or "Hobbesian," or "Lucretian," or "Machiavellian," or "Aristophanean," or "Nietzschean," or "Rousseauian," etc.—not in today's conventional or easily recognizable sense of these affiliations, but in the dramatically new and authentic sense rediscovered in Strauss's mold-breaking recoveries of each thinker's intended comprehensive teaching.

Perhaps nowhere is this characteristic more vivid than in Strauss's most definitive interpretation, *Socrates and Aristophanes.*

There, in an exhaustive study of all the plays of Aristophanes that have come down to us, Strauss refurbishes, reloads, and then fires all the guns of the comprehensive Aristophanean poetic critique of the philosophic life, aiming straight at Strauss's own treasured guide, Socrates — thereby illuminating in an unparalleled way what it means to follow the controversial and challengeable Socratic path.

ANCIENT UTOPIANISM VERSUS MODERN IDEALISM

We may circumscribe the heart of Strauss's reopening of what he called, and what was once well known as, "the quarrel between the ancients and the moderns" by focusing on the contrast Strauss highlights between ancient *utopianism* and its great modern replacement and antagonist, political *idealism* (NRH, 138–39). At the dawn of the modern era, "one of the profoundest students of Plato's *Republic*," the great comedian St. Thomas More, invented the neologism "utopia" (a transliteration of the classical Greek for "good place / no place") as a revealing designation for what is *the* theme of classical political philosophy. "The classic natural right doctrine in its original form, if fully developed, is identical with the doctrine of the best regime" (NRH, 144). But classical political philosophy conceives the "best regime" *not* as an "ideal" to be realized, or even as something to be approached and worked toward; the elaboration of the best regime is intended, rather, as a subtly playful thought-experiment meant to reveal the limitations on what we can expect from all actual political life. In Cicero's lapidary formulation (*De Re Publica* 2.52 — a favorite passage of Strauss), Plato has his Socrates elaborate the regime of the *Republic,* "not as possibly existing, but as making it possible that the principle of political things be seen [*non quae posset esse, sed in qua ratio rerum civilium perspici posset*]." As Strauss himself puts it, concluding his major analysis of Plato: "Socrates makes clear in the *Republic* of what character the city would have to be in order to satisfy the highest need of man. By letting us see that the city constructed in accordance with this requirement is not possible, he lets us see the essential limits, the nature, of the city." A bit earlier in the same essay, Strauss stated this "in a manner which is perhaps more easily intelligible today": "the *Republic* conveys the broadest and deepest analysis of political idealism ever made." Or as Strauss says even more assertively: "certain it is that the *Republic* supplies the most magnificent cure ever devised for every form of political ambition" (CM, 61, 65, 127, 138).

Here it is necessary to interject an inevitably somewhat ponderous didactic comment. Some hasty or superficial commentators on Strauss, having easily discovered that Plato's *Republic* is a work that Strauss is strongly inclined to think teaches the truth about politics, leap to the naive or careless conclusion that Strauss believes in some version of what conventional scholarship claims to be the intention of Plato in the *Republic*. The reigning contemporary scholarly view is that Plato seriously proposed, and even more seriously yearned for, the rule of philosophers ("philosopher-kings"). Accordingly, it has been claimed by some that Strauss, as Plato's modern-day acolyte, and having effected a synthesis of Plato and Nietzsche (!), hoped and worked for the indirect rule of philosophers, as the "powers behind the throne": Strauss is said to have held that he, together with his followers, could achieve power by becoming the sources of some kind of "noble lies," that are presumed to be a sort of semidisguised ideology that would dominate "the cave" of our contemporary "culture." Now the truth about how Strauss understands what he interprets as Plato's intensely ironic work is exactly the opposite—as should become obvious to anyone who is able to discard the blinders that passion or custom puts before the eyes, and who takes the trouble to begin to understand the meaning and the significance, for Strauss, of the quarrel between the ancients and the moderns. Correctly to understand Plato's *Republic* as Strauss understood it (and as Thomas More recapitulated it) is to see that the "noble lie" and the "philosopher-kings" are elaborated therein as culminations of a very rich, and richly thought-provoking, playfulness. To put it bluntly: in Strauss's eyes, such talk of Strauss's synthesis of Nietzsche and Plato is oxymoronic, and reveals a profound ignorance of all three thinkers.

Still, there is of course a good reason why most readers, down through the ages, have drastically underestimated the comedy, and have thereby misunderstood the import, of Plato's great work. Some such misunderstanding was obviously and emphatically intended by Plato (who was assisted, in this regard, by Aristotle's deliciously deadpan criticism of his teacher's book for its impracticality [*Politics*, Bk. 2]—a criticism that features what turns out to be so inaccurate an account of the *Republic*'s contents that it would shame any junior high school student who was asked to summarize what Plato wrote). Even careful and thoughtful readers are only gradually led to become aware of the twinkle in Socrates' eye throughout the dialogue; and Strauss's interpretive studies of Plato to some extent reproduce this coyness (for only gradually does Strauss disclose—and he never discloses with complete explicitness—how thoroughly ironic the Platonic Socrates is in the *Republic*). Why do Plato, and those who understand what he is up to, present his message in so misleading a manner? Why are Plato and Aristotle, and to some extent also Strauss, thus determined to make the *Republic* (and the elaboration of the best regime in other classical works) come to sight as if it conveyed a deadly earnest proposal? There is more than one reason, but the most obvious may be expressed as follows.

A major didactic purpose of the discussion is to induce or to seduce the listeners and the readers to involve their own souls seriously, for a time, in the thought experiment, as something to be lived and struggled through, and not merely observed as in a museum case. This goal—of making the thoughtful reader himself the victim, if you will, of the liberating comedy, would be impaired or defeated if the comic impossibility of the utopia were not kept veiled. Plato's *Republic* may be said to exemplify in consummate fashion the ancient didactic rhetoric that thus draws the very soul of the reader into a dramatic (comic) thought experiment that fully succeeds in transforming the souls of only a very few—those who in some sense live that thought experiment through to its very end. Cicero's *Republic*, Averroës' *Epitome of Plato's Republic*, More's *Utopia*, and other kindred works of genius are free imitations of Plato's *Republic* so understood. What these works have in common is the apparently serious treatment of the impossible as if it were possible. "But the impossible—or a certain kind of the impossible

—if treated as possible is in the highest sense ridiculous or, as we are in the habit of saying, comical. The core of every Aristophanean comedy is something impossible of the kind indicated. The Platonic dialogue brings to its completion what could be thought to have been completed by Aristophanes." As Strauss remarks shortly before this passage, "the Socratic conversation and hence the Platonic dialogue is slightly more akin to comedy than to tragedy. This kinship is noticeable also in Plato's *Republic* which is manifestly akin to Aristophanes' *Assembly of Women*" (CM, 61–62; see also 18).[3]

THE CLASSICAL CONCEPTION OF HUMAN NATURE

The playfully ironic classical teaching on the best regime as utopia reflects and embodies a specific teaching about human nature. Human nature as understood by the Socratics is animated by a profound, passionate longing for self-transcending union with the eternal or divine.[4] This "erotic" yearning is inevitably if obscurely at work everywhere in political action; but this deepest need of the human soul cannot find its clarification and hence its true object through political accomplishment. The erotic longing requires and even elicits purification by reason, inasmuch as man is a thinking being, seeking escape from delusion and illusion. The longing therefore finds its purified or truest expression in the philosophic life and activity. "Man is so built" that his spirit finds its fullest satisfaction only in the life of the essentially private, restless mind, given over to "articulating the riddle of being" (NRH, 75):

Philosophy strives for knowledge of the whole. The whole is the totality of the parts. The whole eludes us but we know parts: we possess partial knowledge of parts. The knowledge which we possess is characterized by a fundamental dualism which has never been overcome. At one pole we find knowledge of homogeneity: above all in arithmetic, but also in other branches of mathematics, and derivatively in all productive arts or crafts. At the opposite pole we find knowledge of heterogeneity, and in particular of heterogeneous ends; the highest form of this kind of knowledge is the art of the statesman and of the educator. The latter kind of knowledge is superior to the former for this reason. As knowledge of the ends of human life, it is knowledge of what makes human life complete or whole; it is therefore knowledge of a whole. Knowledge of the ends of man implies knowledge of the human soul; and the human soul is the only part of the whole which is open to the whole and therefore more akin to the whole than anything else is. But this knowledge—the political art in the highest sense—is not knowledge of *the* whole. It seems that knowledge of the whole would have to combine somehow political knowledge in the highest sense with knowledge of homogeneity. And this combination is not at our disposal. Men are therefore constantly tempted to force the issue by imposing unity on the phenomena, by absolutizing either knowledge of homogeneity or knowledge of ends. Men are constantly attracted and deluded by two opposite charms: the charm of competence which is engendered by mathematics and everything akin to mathematics, and the charm of humble awe, which is engendered by meditation on the human soul and its experiences. Philosophy is characterized by the gentle, if firm, refusal to succumb to either charm. It is the highest form of the mating of courage and moderation. In spite of its highness or nobility, it could appear as Sisyphean or ugly, when one contrasts its achievement with its goal. Yet it is necessarily accompanied, sustained and elevated by *eros*. It is graced by nature's grace. (WIPP, 39–40)

The *eros* which sustains and elevates the genuine philosophic life is then an intellectually and spiritually purified, or indeed purged, *eros*. The nature of this purgation becomes clearer if we follow, with Strauss, the austere treatment of *eros* in Plato's *Republic*. Strauss helps us to see that Plato's *Republic* shows indirectly but with precision why *eros,* after it has been so purified, cannot any longer animate (though it may constructively temper) political ambition and desire for political authority. What a Socratic philosopher contributes to civic life is no more and no less than the "gadfly" stings whose constant irritation counter the city's deep tendency to fall into the dogmatic slumber or lethargy of spiritual self-satisfaction and complacency.

The example and fate of Socrates brings home the parlous implication: the philosopher is per se somewhat deficient in the virtues or capacities required for self-defense, as well as for public service, in an essentially political world (Strauss finds most illuminating in this regard the vivid and subtle contrasts drawn, with a fine hand, by Xenophon between himself and his mentor Socrates). The still more somber consequence is that only a very few individuals can be fortunate enough to surmount the enormous natural obstacles, spiritual as well as material, that stand in the way of the essentially private and unavoidably marginalized life of the mind that is the best life simply. For humankind is primarily not by nature philosophic, or inclined to the philosophic life; rather—to go so far as Aristotle (*Politics* 1253a2–3, 1278b19–30; *Nicomachean Ethics* 1097b11, 1162a17–18)—"the human is by nature a political animal." Humanity's deepest longing, which finds its truest satisfaction only in the life of philosophy, is encased in, penetrated and molded by, a complex concatenation of more immediately felt physical and spiritual needs, personal as well as social. It is chiefly in response to these subphilosophic natural demands that civil society (with its cornerstone the family) and its specific excellences and demands and (partial) fulfillments comes into being.

CLASSICAL REPUBLICAN POLITICAL THEORY

Classical political philosophy is not concerned to rule, but it is concerned to understand, political society—and to share its understanding, in a constructive fashion, with the various political societies and their citizens and rulers. In the pursuit of this civic vocation, classical political theory in the strict or narrow sense takes as its chief task and focus the critical illumination of the highest goals or aspirations that give to political societies their rich and diverse meaningfulness.

Strauss rearticulates the nerve of the classical theory of politics by beginning with a restatement of the classic contention that the most natural political society is not large, anonymous, and open, or heterogeneous (the *ethnos* or "nation"), but is instead small and closed, or homogeneous: the most natural political society is the polis or city, understood as "that complete association which corresponds to the natural range of man's power of knowing and of loving" (NRH, 254n; see also CM, 30–35). Only in the life of an independent city (which is by no means essentially Greek, or even Greco-Roman)[5] is there a good chance that a substantial portion of the members may participate directly and in a fraternal spirit in the spiritually enlarging challenges of shaping the collective destiny—as rulers, but also, and more widely, as ruled but responsive, deeply involved, and responsible citizens.

The city so understood "antedates the distinction between state and society and cannot therefore be put together out of 'state' and 'society'"; the city as conceived in classical political theory is emphatically not a "city-state." The distinction between state (as the realm of necessary, and necessarily unattractive, coercion) and society (as the realm of free flourishing) that is so fundamental to our modern conceptual framework is based on a radical demotion, arising in and out of modern political theory, of the status in human life of politics—of the sphere of coercive law, of collective deliberation, and of authoritative decision. More precisely, it is a massive tendency of modern thought to attempt to conceive of politics as pertaining to something called the state, which "must be indifferent to virtue and vice as such, as distinguished from transgressions of the state's laws which have no other function than the protection of the life, liberty, and property of each citizen." But the city, as conceived in the Socratic theory that grows out of deep reflection on classical republican life, is the locus of that materially self-sufficient living together that most truly suits human nature. The city "is the most comprehensive and the highest society since it aims at the highest and most comprehensive good at which any society can aim." "This highest good is happiness," understood as centered on "the practice of virtue and primarily of moral virtue": "the chief purpose of the city is the noble life and therefore the chief concern of the city must be the virtue of its members and hence liberal education" (CM, 30–31).[6]

The city at its best is thus "liberal," in the classic sense of the term (*eleutheros*): that is, decisively influenced by "the morally serious" (*spoudaioi*), the "gentlemen" (*kaloikagathoi*), who possess the moral and civic virtues aimed at (though by no means automatically produced) by a truly liberating or "*liberal* education" (*paideia eleutheria*). In its original, natural form such a genuinely liberal education proceeds by "familiar intercourse" with "elder statesmen," by "receiving instruction from paid teachers in the art of speaking," by "reading histories and books of travel, by meditating on the works of the poets" ("the fountains of that education"), and, "of course by taking part in political life." "All this requires leisure on the part of youths as well as on the part of their elders"; it is the preserve of "wealth of a certain kind: a kind of wealth the administration of which, to say nothing of its acquisition, does not take up much of [one's] time" (LAM, 10–11).

As Strauss stresses, classical republicanism recognizes that this essential economic basis of the liberally educated (their privately owned, inherited land) implies an insuperable defect in the justice of their rule: "only the accident of birth decides whether a given individual has a chance of becoming a gentlemen or will necessarily become a villain; hence aristocracy is unjust." It does not follow, however, that democracy is more just, for its economic basis subjects it to an even more serious moral flaw: a corruption of justice as the common good of society. Strauss quotes in this connection Rousseau's *Social Contract* (3.4): "If there were a people consisting of gods, it would rule itself democratically. A government of such perfection is not suitable for human beings." Democracy likes to flatter itself as being the rule of all, but in fact democracy means rule by the majority, who in all actual human societies are the unleisured and uneducated, or at best the illiberally educated —"because they have to work for their livelihood and to rest so that they can work the next day." The majority view education not chiefly in terms of its liberality, or its potential to liberate the mind, but instead in terms of its economic utility. In their needy (or even wealthy) lack of experience of a life preoccupied with the striving after virtue, the majority are overwhelmingly prone to make, not virtue or human excellence their society's goal, but instead material prosperity and "freedom as a right of every citizen to live as he likes." The workers when citizens do make a substantial civic contribution. They form the backbone of the militia. They can become vigilant watchdogs against oppression. Similarly, the rich contribute wealth and knowledge of its acquisition and management. But unlike the morally serious, the majority (including the rich as well as the poor) tend to "praise virtue as a means for acquiring wealth and honor"; they do not reliably "regard virtue as choiceworthy for its own sake" (LAM, 4–5, 12).

To be sure, it is also apparent to classical theory that "the existing aristocracies proved to be oligarchies, rather than aristocracies." Certainly "for all practical purposes," the classics "were satisfied with a regime in which the gentlemen share power with the people in such a way that the people elect the magistrates and the council from among the gentlemen and demand an account of them at the end of their term of office." "A variation of this thought" is "the notion of the mixed regime." The mixed regime is far from being perfectly just, but, if well structured, it can repress some of the characteristic vices, and promote some virtues, of both the rich and the poor. But it is crucial that, as much as possible, the small minority of the morally serious, the gentlemen, set the tone.[7] Strauss denies "Aristotle's alleged anti-democratic prejudice": "the democracy with which he takes issue is the democracy of the city, not modern democracy"; "modern democracy would have to be described with a view to its intention from Aristotle's point of view as a mixture of democracy and aristocracy."[8]

THE FUNDAMENTAL TENSION

There is by no means a harmony, though, between the virtues and demands of the life of the gentleman-citizen or statesman, and the virtues and demands of the contemplative life. On the contrary: between the two there exists a mutually dangerous, though not unfruitful, tension. The tension is heightened, paradoxically, by the Socratic philosopher's appreciation of the evident power in the claims, and especially in the divine claims, belonging to the civic virtues.[9] For this appreciation compels the philosopher to justify his apparently strange way of life, with its inner detachment from civil society and with its claim to transcend the gentlemanly virtues. The only nondogmatic and therefore satisfyingly convincing justification must be one that reasons strictly on the basis of premises not specific to philosophers but belonging to or shared by the nonphilosophic or prephilosophic.[10] The Socratic philosopher must therefore undertake a severely self-questioning, emotionally trying, and necessarily protracted, or indeed never-terminated, argumentative dialogue with the most articulate and open-minded adherents and advocates of the morally serious political life.[11]

The Socratic dialogues take place characteristically with self-selected young—who, despite or even because of their political talents and ambition, still have the free time and the passionate openness that enables them to engage in what, from society's or their fathers' perspective, may well appear to be at best a waste of time and energy. The Socratic dialectic is "the attempt to lead the qualified citizens, or rather their qualified sons, from the political life to the philosophic life" (WIPP, 93–94). The success of the Socratic dialectic entails the "conversion [turning around] of the soul," as Socrates terms it (*Republic* 518c–d), of a few of these highly promising young. These "conversions" provide decisive evidence that the spiritual purification that Socrates himself once underwent, as a consequence of his thinking through of his own prephilosophic opinions about the noble and the just, was not idiosyncratic. These conversions are the core of Socratic political philosophy, which provides the foundation or ground of philosophy simply. Yet these conversions are not welcome to parents or to the authorities of civic education, who are strongly inclined to interpret them as "corrupting the young." "Precisely the best of the non-philosophers, the good citizens," are "passionately opposed to philosophy (*Republic* 517a)" (CM, 125).

This reaction is understandable. For the Socratic perscrutation of civic life does indeed expose serious contradictions in the most authoritative, even the gentlemanly, civic opinions about justice and nobility. The Socratic critique can be mistakenly taken to be a denigration—rather than a transcendence—of civic life.[12] Moreover, as Aristophanes made so comically (and therefore not too dangerously) vivid in his *Clouds,* Socratic interrogation or skepticism courts the risk of becoming confused with sophistic skepticism, thereby weakening the citizenry's attachment to authoritative moral and religious opinions, whose deep-rooted, habitual, or tradition-grounded hold on the heart is an essential basis for healthy politics, especially in public-spirited republican society (see esp. CM, 21–25). In short, there is something truly dangerous to society, to rulers and to ruled, in the Socratic inquiry and dialectic; and so it is no accident that there arises, in response, a counter-threat, to Socratic philosophy, from the self-preservative instincts of even or precisely a relatively healthy republican society. "Philosophy as such" is "suspect" to "the majority of men."[13]

THE CLASSIC MEANING OF "ESOTERIC WRITING"

Socratic political philosophizing is therefore compelled to respond to this twofold danger, and to take responsibility for mitigating it. The response takes the form of a carefully worked out art of public communication, oral and written. The aim of this art's benevolent "deception" (see esp. Plato's *Phaedrus* 261e–262b) is to blunt the potentially harmful effects of Socratic questioning while stressing the constructive contribution Socratic wisdom can make to the edification of the civic virtues. The dialogues of Plato are the supreme examples of the Socratic art of writing.[14] Authentic Socratic writing always proceeds on at least two massive levels: what Strauss, following modern as well as ancient guides, termed the "exoteric" and the "esoteric."

The latter, the deeper and more hidden level,[15] is intended to arouse and to initiate a few of the strongest among the young, or young at heart—by a process of increasingly more challenging puzzles, the more arresting of which stare out from the very surface of the writing. The most serious concern of this esoteric dimension of Socratic writing is to keep alive the enactment of the Socratic dialectic and the witnessing of its soul-transforming consequences. Yet the extraordinary difficulty in doing so—in finding and then arousing the very few truly capable readers—makes even this deepest level of writing inevitably a form of playful hope against hope (see Plato's *Phaedrus* 275c-277b).

The more palpable, exoteric level (or levels) of such writing exhibits what Maimonides characterizes as a divine "wily graciousness." It draws attention away from the most troubling aspects of the ladder of challenges conveyed by the deeper, esoteric level, and delivers a message that is meant to illuminate and to put in the foreground the genuine though limited human greatness of which politics is susceptible; at the same time, this exoteric level of Socratic writing aims to enrich and to enlarge religious faith, through "theology" that conveys something of what philosophy has discovered about the truly eternal or divine: "political philosophy is the indispensable handmaid of theology" (CM, 1).

Yet the art of esoteric/exoteric communication is further complicated: even the message that teaches about political greatness and what can be known by reason about the truly divine cannot be presented altogether openly—because of the unhappily pervasive presence of tyranny in political life. The human aspirations to partake of the divine, to achieve excellence and to live honorably and hence honored, are susceptible to terrible perversions. Tyranny assumes many guises, not always easy to penetrate. In most if not all times and places, the Socratics find themselves dwelling in societies under the thumb of more or less tyrannical rulers, usually dominating in the name of various narrow and narrowing orthodoxies. The philosopher will need to struggle to elude persecution, while unmasking tyranny—not only or mainly for himself, but especially for all those whom he wishes to reach and to teach by his public communication, both philosophic and republican. Socratic philosophers' writings intended to remain alive in many unrepublican times and places in the far and alien future are therefore designed to give the exaggerated impression of preaching obedience and conformity—generally, but also specifically (in relation to the powers that be in the writer's own time and place).[16] Only "between the lines" do such writings disclose ironic critiques of orthodoxy, including "aristocracy" and religious tyranny, in its local but also in its typical or even universal penchants. These covertly subversive critiques are meant to help many readers to begin to learn techniques of writing and speaking by which freedom of critical thinking—not only philosophic, but also civic republican—can survive "underground" (awaiting the rare chance to resurface) in all sorts of more or less oppressive regimes. Accordingly, Strauss's major works that teach about esoteric and exoteric writing are entitled *"Persecution and the Art of Writing"* and *"On Tyranny."*

We must hasten to add that the meaning and purpose of esoteric writing undergo a considerable transformation in modern political philosophy, inasmuch as the latter has a crucially different, if derivative, understanding of the relation between philosophy and society, or between theory and practice. This entails a distinctly modern version of philosophic rhetoric or of the philosophic strategy of communication. In the next chapter we will introduce Strauss's understanding of the precise character of these important differences.

Strauss was led to rediscover the lost ancient art of writing, and thus the forgotten core of classical political philosophy, in part by his early intense study of the great Platonic political theorists living within the world of medieval Islam and Judaism—especially al-Fārābī and Maimonides. And Strauss eventually confirmed, through his study and interpretation of Marsilius of Padua, that authentic Platonic-Aristotelian thinking and esoteric writing was successfully revived in Christendom as well as in the world of Islam. The writings of these medieval political philosophers were of crucial help to Strauss because of what appeared at first to be the epochal contrast between their historical context, dominated by biblical scripture and scriptural law, and the apparently altogether different historical context of Plato himself, living in a pagan world dominated by the poets. Strauss came to learn from these medievals, in each of the three great revealed religions, that, and how, they had, by grasping the hand held out to them by Plato, transcended their historical context through discovering within it the permanent problems originally uncovered by Plato within his context. It was through this discovery of the continuing decisive power, within each of the three great religious dispensations, of the Platonic theologico-political understanding that

Strauss was enabled to see or to uncover the most important trans-historical significance of Socratic political philosophy (see esp. PAW). These medieval writings were what originally opened the younger Strauss's eyes to the supreme question animating and pre-occupying Socratic philosophy: "the theologico-political problem" —which, Strauss declares in one of his pithy published autobio-graphical statements near the end of his life, "has remained *the* theme of my investigations" (PHPW).

Strauss's rediscovery of esoteric writing is intended by him to be his revolutionary contribution to "the sociology of knowledge" (PAW, beginning). By the same token, this rediscovery is the core of Strauss's revolutionary suggestion about the proper understand-ing of the relation to their historical contexts of those thinkers who employ such writing. Strauss's rediscovery is intended, among other things, to provide the empirical evidence that refutes or draws radically into doubt today's reigning scholarly framework for understanding the relation of philosophic thought to histori-cal context. The upholders and defenders of today's prevailing view have not yet begun to face the devastating implications of this em-pirical historical evidence that is revealed and explained by the ap-plication of Strauss's thesis on esoteric writing. And it is easy to understand why contemporary scholars, and especially our intel-lectual historians, have done everything they can to dodge this confrontation. For it explodes much of their lives' work. Confront-ing this suggestion—even in order to try to refute it adequately —would force contemporary scholars to engage in an elaborate "retooling." The fanatically obscurantist response of conventional scholars has been to denounce the thesis of esoteric writing con-cerning the relation of thought to historical context while simulta-neously if incoherently proclaiming the myth that Strauss and his followers ignore historical context in their interpretations of past thinkers.

The reigning contemporary scholarly hypothesis or claim con-cerning the relation of philosophic thought to its historical context is most succinctly expressed in the following words that Strauss quotes from his critic, the historicist scholar of political theory George Sabine: "there are presumptions implicit in what Carl

Becker called the 'climate of opinion' of an age that no contemporary ever fully grasps, precisely because they are so deeply engrained in the texture of his thinking."[17] The empirical evidence that Strauss assembles in and through his meticulous textual interpretations proves, on the contrary, that a tiny minority of those writers[18] whose books have come down to us became fully self-conscious of and radically critical about all of the most deeply ingrained presumptions of their respective epochs, and thus liberated their truest thinking and teaching entirely from the limitations of their particular historical contexts. Strauss shows that these few truly liberated thinkers succeeded in attaining and conveying in writing final knowledge of the permanent and transhistorical problems; they did so while simultaneously devising a comprehensive strategy of communication that allowed each of them to pass, in the eyes of the vast majority of their readers, as conforming in decisive respects—not only to passionate prejudices that dominated their own time, but to certain crucial, and more deeply rooted, moral prejudices that pervade every time. While it is practically nigh impossible for such writers to avoid entirely opprobrium, ostracism, and persecution (including book burning), they are nonetheless able, by the strategy of esoteric writing, to substantially mitigate these evils, for themselves and for their intended students or best readers.

Strauss does not deny that in order to understand even a truly liberated and liberating thinker's text that was written in an epoch distant from our own we sometimes need, in widely varying degrees, the supplement of certain kinds of historical information not provided by the author: "the need for extraneous information derives from the fact that a man's foresight as to what could be intelligible to posterity is necessarily limited"; in some cases —Spinoza is the standout example—there may even be a "background" that, from the author's point of view, is "indispensable for the understanding of his books, but could not reasonably be supplied through his books, because no one can say everything without being tedious to everyone." But "this means that in his work of reconstruction the interpreter must follow the signposts erected by" the author "himself," and, only "secondarily, the indications that" the author "left accidentally in his writings." In the case of the few texts that exhibit marks of truly profound strategic self-consciousness about their historical context, "we must never lose sight of the fact that information of this [latter] kind cannot have more than a strictly subordinate function, or that such information is to be integrated into a framework authentically or explicitly supplied by" the author—rather than a framework invented by today's scholarship. "Extraneous knowledge can never be permitted to supply the clue to" an author's "teaching except after it has been proved beyond any reasonable doubt that it is impossible to make head and tail of his teaching as he presented it." For "every deviation from that principle exposes one to the danger that one tries to understand" the thinker in question "better than he understood himself before one has understood him as he understood himself; it exposes one to the danger that one understands," not the thinker or his thought, "but a figment of one's imagination."[19]

We must constantly struggle against the almost overwhelming temptation—pressed upon us by all versions of "respectable" current opinion—that we are somehow in possession of an understanding of the "context," including the author's intellectual biography, that is more important than the self-consciously intended information that the author gives us in his text. Thus, for example, there is no surer way to block access to learning what Plato intended to teach than to interpret his dialogues in the light of what is supposed to be known or surmised about their chronological order of composition, and hence what that chronology reveals about Plato's "development" as a thinker—something about which the dialogues themselves, and Plato's remarks about the writing of the dialogues in his letters, indicate not the slightest sign of interest. In studying the rare cases of authorial minds from the past whose liberation appears to be complete, we need to learn to see the author's historical environment exactly as he saw it and conveyed it to his alert and demanding readers. We need to identify the "context" with what the author indicates is his context. Above all, Strauss stresses, we need to figure out, from what the author communicates to his best intended readers, precisely which were the diverse intended audiences of the author, and what were the distinct rhetorical strategies the author self-consciously adopted in order to deal with his widely dissimilar intended audiences.

In this regard we need to learn to consider "historical context" from a far broader, as well as a more elevated, point of view than is nowadays conventionally supposed. We need to achieve a more elevated conception of historical context, because we must learn to view the environment not as necessarily shaping every thinker, even in the sense of being that to which his thought fundamentally responds: instead, we need to consider whether we are not in the presence of a thinker for whom his immediate environment was a sort of prison from which he executed a most elaborate and largely undetected escape—not only for himself but also, in varying degrees, for a few fellow inmates. We need a far broader conception of context, because we must recognize that the few truly liberated authors do not write solely or even chiefly with a view to the peculiarities of the audience of their immediate historico-cultural environment. While never being so foolish as to forget the rhetorical demands of concealment imposed by the specific powerful prejudices reigning in their own times, these authors mean to write books that will be, in Thucydides' lapidary words, "a possession for all times" (*History of the Peloponnesian War* 1.24.4). Now (Strauss observes) "the flight to immortality requires an extreme discretion in the selection of one's luggage" (PAW, 160). The authors in question therefore bend their efforts to devising a rhetoric that not only conciliates the authoritative prejudices peculiar to their own times, but, still more, accommodates itself to the abiding prejudices, or deep sources of prejudice, that the authors are convinced will be expressed by human nature in all times and places (if in varying degrees). Simultaneously, they leave behind clues that allow an alert and demanding reader gradually to become fully cognizant of this complex dual level of strategy and, more important, of the historical and eternal human characteristics that dictate this strategy. Perhaps the supreme expression of this complex teaching is Plato's *Phaedrus,* interpreted as a whole.

Yet it is "impossible even for the most far-sighted man to foresee which pseudo-philosophies will emerge, and gain control of the minds of men in the future" (PAW, 155). The actualization of the long-term rhetorical strategy of the most liberated and liberating writers therefore requires a decisive "contribution" from their potentially most liberatable readers and commentators in each time and place. In our age in particular, uniquely darkened as it is by the loss of even the memory of esoteric writing, a peculiarly great and rare effort is required—and Strauss, in and through his own unprecedented art of writing, means to supply the crucial foundation of that effort. In our age, the reading of the most liberating because liberated books requires a constant movement back and forth between what we begin to learn from those books and a self-critical reflection on what they imply about the drastic deficiencies of the "pseudo-philosophies" that initially dominate our own thinking: "not indeed philosophy, but the way in which the introduction to philosophy must proceed, necessarily changes with the change in the artificial or accidental obstacles to philosophy. The artificial obstacles may be so strong at a given time that a most elaborate 'artificial' introduction has to be completed before the 'natural' introduction can begin. It is conceivable that a particular pseudo-philosophy may emerge whose power cannot be broken but by the most intensive reading of old books." Strauss goes on to suggest that "the dominant thought of the present age" may "have to be described" as "a pseudo-philosophy of this kind" (PAW, 155).

Not only does Strauss assemble crucial evidence that renders dubious contemporary scholarship's reigning historicist conception of the relation of the few greatest writers to their historical context or milieu; in addition, Strauss shows precisely how it is that our contemporary historicist assumption actually works, psychologically, to block the mind of the historian or scholar from being able easily to apprehend or even to look for the most relevant empirical counterevidence invalidating his basic historicist assumption. In other words, Strauss takes the further step of explaining a major reason why (apart from the simple brute strength of groupthink) those upholding the contemporary scholarly consensus that he is refuting cling so close-mindedly and even desperately to their empirically indefensible methodological assumption concerning the relation of the most liberated thinking to its historical milieu. The essence of Strauss's explanation goes as follows.

Historicism (or the mind of the historicist scholar) "assumes" that "every philosophy is essentially the expression of its time"; and "it makes this assumption the basis of its interpretation of classical philosophy." But classical philosophy "claimed to teach *the* truth, and not merely the truth of classical Greece." So, the historicist is in the position of *beginning* by assuming, without question, and in such a way as to rule out questioning, that classical philosophy is *wrong* in the decisive sense. The typical scholar of our time assumes without even being fully conscious of the assumption that he is decisively superior in knowledge to, that he knows the decisive thing better than, all the great thinkers he studies. Now on such a basis, he cannot ever really open himself to the nonhistoricist thinkers he is studying, or listen to them with an open mind (NIPPP, 330–31). What is more, since the intellectual historian "knows in advance" that the philosophic thought that he is trying to understand is in the decisive sense "false, he lacks the incentive for studying that doctrine with sympathy or care." In particular, the historian is deaf to the implications of the repeated indications by the greatest classical philosophers of a vast gulf in wisdom between them, in their knowledge of the human situation, and the rest of humanity—a gulf that is due to the fact that the latter live immersed in spiritual loyalty to societies whose essential medium, foundation, and sustenance is a mesh of opinion that is hostile to the purgative medicine of critical reason. But, Strauss underlines, from this ignored message of the classical philosophers, if or when this message is received and understood, the conclusion that they engaged in esoteric writing "necessarily follows" (WIPP, 227, 229; also 68).

Let us not fail to observe that, by thus explaining this debilitating scotoma induced in contemporary historians of thought by their historicist premises, Strauss is in effect showing that, and how, the blinding disease might be cured: he is trying to help the historian, whom he so critically and bracingly addresses, to undertake a self-cure. After all, Strauss himself began as an historian of thought who, whatever his philosophic motives and ambitions, was originally still under the spell of the historicism on which he was raised (the powerful vestiges are apparent in Strauss's first book, SCR). In a statement that I am inclined to think includes an autobiographical element, Strauss writes, in praise of a noble potential hidden within the contemporary academic discipline of the history of philosophy (PAW, 158): "The study of earlier thought, if conducted with intelligence and assiduity, leads to a revitalization of earlier ways of thinking. The historian who started out with the conviction that true understanding of human thought is understanding of every teaching in terms of its particular time or as an expression of its particular time, necessarily familiarizes himself with the view, constantly urged upon him by his subject matter, that his initial conviction is unsound. More than that: he is brought to realize that one cannot understand the thought of the past as long as one is guided by that initial conviction. This self-destruction of historicism is not altogether an unforeseen result."

STRAUSS'S PECULIAR HISTORICAL SITUATION

In Strauss's critique of contemporary historical scholarship rooted in historicist assumptions, there becomes visible a deep, if deeply self-conscious, complication in Strauss's own position (and in the position of those who perspicaciously follow his lead). The complication appears when we remark that Strauss's quest (for a fully open-minded recovery of the true teaching intended by classical philosophy—with a view to reopening and judging anew the quarrel of the ancients and the moderns) is, as a necessarily and essentially historical quest, by no means a simply or directly classical project. Strauss stresses that classical philosophy in its pristine form was not concerned with the history of thought as such—"however much philosophers might have appreciated reports on earlier thought in their absolutely ancillary function" (PAW, 157–58; WIPP, 73–77). He points out that even or precisely the most philosophic of all ancient historians, Thucydides, does not consider it appropriate to devote a single line to the history of thought—or to intellectual, cultural, or religious history; history, for Thucydides, means strictly political history—from which he derives and conveys knowledge of man's permanent place in the whole, knowledge that is transhistorical or "a possession for all times." As for Socrates himself, Xenophon reports him saying that he led his friends in reading groups that studied "the treasures that the wise men of old left behind in the books that they wrote" (*Memorabilia* 1.6.14); but the clear implication of this report is that Socrates listened to and reflected questioningly upon these texts pretty much as he did in reaction to the speeches of enlightened contemporaries. As for the opinions that Socrates sought to cross-examine—the opinions containing "the most elementary premises" that reveal the "problems of justice" and other "permanent problems"—they were also, and more readily, available to Socrates immediately, in his surrounding contemporary lifeworld.

Strauss's situation is drastically different, and self-consciously so. Strauss therefore stresses that, insofar as he is inclined to think that the classics may be fundamentally correct, it follows that much of his own historical researches are necessary because, *and only because,* he has the ill fortune to be born in "an age of decline or decay"—an historical epoch that is artificially estranged from, nay, that even blocks, the natural route toward the truth about man's place in the whole (CPH, 576, 585). Our historical condition, from the point of view of access to the fundamental problems as grasped by the classics, is what Strauss (modifying the famous Platonic metaphor) christens "the pit beneath the cave" (PL, Introd., n. 2; PAW, 154–56). It is true that this needs to be immediately qualified, inasmuch as the crisis of our times has shaken or cracked the walls of our "pit" to a degree that has not been seen for generations—since the time, at the turn of the nineteenth century, when the historicist dogma began to congeal the Western mind. Strauss goes so far as to say: "The genuine understanding of the political philosophies which is then necessary may be said to have been rendered possible by the shaking of all traditions; the crisis of our time may have the accidental advantage of enabling us to understand in an untraditional or fresh manner what was hitherto understood only in a traditional or derivative manner. This may apply especially to classical political philosophy which has been seen for a considerable time only through the lenses of modern political philosophy and its various successors" (CM, 9). Nevertheless, our liberation from our "pit beneath the cave" requires not only a study of the classics but a simultaneous or intermingled enormous effort to become fully aware of the medieval and modern traditions—of theological, philosophic, and to some extent political developments—that have issued in the artificially reconfigured and mutilated "common sense" and scholarly distortion of the classics that mars vision in our epoch.

Yet Strauss's historical situation, and the situation of anyone who follows him, is still more complicated than this. We not only need to struggle to find our way to a critical perspective on our artificial, because theoretically reconstructed, lifeworld ("the pit beneath the cave"), so as to find access to the original, natural, unconstructed lifeworld (the Platonic "cave"), and thence to partaking of the Socratic ascent from that cave. We also, insofar as we succeed in these latter tasks, must constantly move from what we discover to be the power of ancient and classically inspired medieval thought back to the various versions of the great modern critiques of the ancients and medievals, testing to see which of the two grand parties to the quarrel between the ancients and the moderns is more persuasive in its claims. Moreover, we are impelled to this renewal or reenactment of the quarrel by the peculiar crisis of our times, of whose solution, by way of a recovery of either ancient or original modern rationalism, we are far from being entirely confident. I believe that Strauss, for his part, never ceases to entertain, and to wrestle with, the possibility that the crucial claimed insights of radical historicism might be in a decisive sense sound.

Strauss teaches that we find ourselves, then, in a position that demands a dauntingly severe and yet flexible intellectual probity. We struggle to liberate ourselves from the authority of current scholarly conventions in order to study classical political philosophy with true candor; yet we must be wary of becoming, as a consequence, so overwhelmed by the power of classical philosophy that we are bewitched into believing that we know Socrates is right before we actually do have such knowledge. We must strive accordingly to make sure that we have not underestimated the power of modern thought, in all or any of its diverse successive manifestations—even as we keep keen our awareness of the need to liberate ourselves entirely from any enchantment with or by modern thought. We have to resist the temptation to a self-forgetting and thus consoling romanticist or antiquarian plunge into the classics as a way of ceasing to think about the crisis of our times or the historicist challenge; yet we must prevent our most urgent need, our need to confront and to resolve that crisis, from coloring our study, from polluting the purity with which we open ourselves to the classics. "The return to classical political philosophy is both necessary and tentative or experimental. Not in spite but because of its tentative character, it must be carried out seriously, i.e.[,] without squinting at our present predicament. There is no danger that we can ever become oblivious of this predicament since it is the incentive to our whole concern with the classics" (CM, 11).

3 : The Rediscovery and Reassessment
of the Foundations of Modernity

n bringing back to light the full import and importance of the theologico-political problem, Strauss brought back to light the deepest cause of the break that "the moderns" effected with "the ancients." In Strauss's interpretation, the philosophers who initiated and elaborated distinctively modern rationalism and republicanism (Machiavelli, Bacon, Hobbes, Descartes, Spinoza, Locke, Montesquieu) were moved by public-spirited dissatisfaction with the utopian conservatism or lack of political ambition of ancient political philosophy. For this lack of enterprise, in their eyes, left social existence too much at the mercy of theocracy in one form or another (see, e.g., Plato's *Laws*). Still worse, this philosophic outlook conceded to the claimants of revelation that the human spirit was so constituted as irrepressibly to long for a transcendence of secular social existence. And this appeared to leave unshaken—nay, even could be used, and was used, to strengthen—the claimed evidence of the experience of divine revelations demanding the chastening or sacrifice, the subordination and thus (in the modern rationalists' eyes) mutilation, of human reason and rational social felicity. The modern rationalists rebelled. They sought and claimed to find a superior resolution of the theologico-political problem. They did so through attempting a wholesale reconception of the human condition and its prospects—initiating a comprehensive theoretical and practical project that has yet to reach a satisfactory conclusion.

THE MODERN REVOLT

Strauss sums up the unifying core of "the modern project" as: "the secular movement which tries to guarantee the actualization of the ideal, or to prove the necessary coincidence of the rational and the real, or to get rid of that which essentially transcends every possible human reality" (WIPP, 51; as for the deepest philosophic goal motivating this movement, see PL, Introd.). Strauss thus sees modern "idealism" and modern "realism" as revolving in twin orbits around one another. In the modern perspectives, whether idealistic or realistic, humanity is no longer to be conceived in terms of a hierarchy of spiritual needs directed by and toward a natural perfection or order of rank within the soul. Instead, what is to be regarded as natural to the human species are animal passions, the strongest of which are the drive for security and the drive for superiority or control, given scope in a uniquely human plasticity that is shapeable and hence shaped by reason, which can figure out an integration of the passions. Mankind can and should devise for itself artificial structures of existence that allow the most gratifying expression of its passions, rendered human through conscious and unconscious construction and reconstruction. Viewing modernity synoptically, Strauss saw it as exhibiting a historical-dialectical drama of a never-fully-accomplished and ever-more-radical effort to complete an account of the human essence or condition that would provide worldly standards of aspiration for human action, guided by reason — or, eventually, guided no longer by reason but instead by a supra- or subrational but still secular and thus nontranscendent "historical process." However intense are the mutual disagreements among the different stages and philosophic giants of modernity, all share a defining common ground in the rejection of the key elements in the classical outlook.

At the highest and decisive level, the modern doctrines in one way or another all abandon the classical contention that human nature is directed toward the mind's pursuit of knowledge of nature and the whole for its own sake, launched by the erotic longing for eternity: "oblivion of eternity, or, in other words, estrangement from man's deepest desire and therewith from the primary issues, is the price which modern man had to pay, from the very beginning, for attempting to be absolutely sovereign, to become the master and owner of nature, to conquer chance" (WIPP, 55). In the various modern schemes, the needs that animate human nature are conceived as satisfiable in and through a well-constructed society, supplemented by humanistic "education" and various sorts of personal "psychological" regimen. Philosophy is to serve and to guide, i.e., to rule indirectly, such a society with such education and such regimens.

This requires the radical reconception, not only of philosophy itself and of its political role, but of civic and personal spiritual health. In the modern perspective, in contrast to the ancient, morality and religion are to be properly understood, and gradually reshaped, as "civil" and as personally liberating; what goes beyond, or, still worse, conflicts with, social well-being and personal freedom is to be hived off and jettisoned as unnatural and unnecessary "fanaticism" or "superstition." Simultaneously, in the modern perspective, in contrast to the ancient, the distinctiveness and decisive superiority of philosophy as a way of life, as an existential transformation or "conversion of the soul," becomes in various degrees obscured. For the ancients, the "definition of political philosophy" according to which " 'philosophy' indicates the manner of treatment," while " 'political' indicates both the subject matter and function," is only "provisional"; according to the "deeper meaning" of "political philosophy," "the adjective 'political' in the expression 'political philosophy' designates not so much a subject matter as a manner of treatment; from this point of view, I say, 'political' philosophy means primarily not the philosophic treatment of politics, but the political, or popular, treatment of philosophy, or the political introduction to philosophy" (WIPP, 10–11, 14, 93; see also Tarcov, 1983b, 19). For classical philosophy precedes classical political philosophy, not only in time but in rank. Political philosophy, centered on the critical conversational analysis of the just and the noble as expressed in prephilosophic authoritative opinions, comes into being chiefly to defend, to justify, and to ground philosophy—as the way of life of the truly awakened human, open most fully to the whole, and consumed by the unfinished and unfinishable quest for final knowledge of the natural order and, most centrally, of human nature, its place and its fate in the whole.

In modern political philosophy, this "deeper meaning" of political philosophy is first blurred or obscured (Machiavelli) and then progressively lost from view. Starting at least with Hobbes, modern political philosophy proceeds on the working assumption, or accepts "on trust," that political philosophy is "possible or necessary" (NRH, 167). Modern political philosophy no longer sees its raison d'être to be the justification of the necessity and possibility of philosophy to and in the terms of prephilosophic opinion. From its very inception, modern political philosophy is, to say the least, far less concerned with the careful articulation of, and then the painstaking dialectical ascent from, the thoughtful commonsense opinions of citizens and statesmen, especially about the noble and the just in the fullest sense (righteousness). Modern political philosophy is much more impressed and preoccupied with the deeds than with the speeches or self-understanding of political life. Modern political philosophy, like modern philosophy, begins from a radical doubt of common sense and its opinions, and proceeds to replace or to supersede those opinions with apparently indubitable, universally self-evident first principles—inferred from the deeds more than the speeches of political life—from which the whole of a new, truly reasonable or truly effective (and thus self-vindicating) moral and political universe can be constructed.

THE TRANSFORMED MEANING
OF "ESOTERIC WRITING"

There is in practice, then, no insuperable tension between philosophy and society, in the modern scheme. The Socratic dialectic becomes apparently superfluous. So, the meaning of "esotericism" (benevolently deceptive writing) undergoes a profound modification (see esp. PAW, 32–35). In the classical framework, reenacted especially by the medieval philosophers living under Judaism and Islam, esoteric writing is the device by which an essentially and forever dissident philosophic minority constructively shields itself and society from a potentially destructive mutual intimacy:

The precarious status of philosophy in Judaism as well as in Islam was not in every respect a misfortune for philosophy. The official recognition of philosophy in the Christian world made philosophy subject to ecclesiastical supervision. The precarious position of philosophy in the Islamic-Jewish world resembled in this respect its status in classical Greece. . . . Even the philosophic schools were founded by men without authority, by private men. The Islamic and Jewish philosophers recognized the similarity between this state of things and the one prevailing in their own time. Elaborating on some remarks of Aristotle, they compared the philosophic life to the life of the hermit. (PAW, 21)

Esotericism is, for the classical philosophers, one may say, the way they avoid the danger of a mutual contamination and corruption of politics and philosophy. In modern rationalism, by contrast, esotericism from the very beginning includes in addition —and is transformed by—a program of most subtle propaganda aimed at manipulating the unphilosophic leaders, and even the mass, of the citizenry so as to make them subject, indirectly and in part unawares, to a ruling philosophic or quasi-philosophic elite and their project of secularization (see TOM). The eventual result was a degeneration, through which the ancient art of rhetoric was more and more swamped and finally extinguished by the new art of propaganda. Modern philosophy became justifiably subject to the suspicion that it might be motivated not so much by the will to truth as by the will to power. Some of the philosophers themselves lost clear sight of the radical difference between their doctrinal dogmas and the underlying philosophic skepticism or quest for knowledge of the whole that defines philosophy as such. Modern political philosophy more and more deliberately allowed itself to play a major role in spawning world-historical revolutions. So-called philosophers and political theorists have finally not been ashamed to embrace arrant, vulgar propaganda, including sloganeering.[1] In the late-modern, and all-too-common worst cases, tyranny itself was supported, rather than subverted, by what called itself theory. Transmogrified into the monstrosity called "ideology," political "theory" was not ashamed to become the sponsor of "ideological" mass political parties or movements (fascists, socialists, nationalists, Marxists, Nazis, Baathists, Islamicists, etc., etc.). As Strauss expressed it in his book *On Tyranny,* we have been "brought face to face with"

> a kind of tyranny that surpassed the boldest imagination of the most powerful thinkers of the past. . . . In contradistinction to classical tyranny, present-day tyranny has at its disposal "technology" as well as "ideology"; more generally expressed, it presupposes the existence of "science," i.e., of a particular interpretation, or kind, of science. Conversely, classical tyranny, unlike modern tyranny, was confronted, actually or potentially, by a science which was not meant to be applied to the "conquest of nature" or to be popularized and diffused. . . . Confronted by the appalling alternative that man, or human thought, must be collectivized either by one stroke and without mercy or else by slow and gentle processes, we are forced to wonder how we could escape from this dilemma. We reconsider therefore the elementary and unobtrusive conditions of human freedom. (OT, 23, 27)

ASSESSING MODERN LIBERAL DEMOCRACY

Still, there is an enormous, and politically most significant, difference between the earlier, and more moderate, expression of the modern project, and its later, ever more desperate waves. The experience of twentieth-century politics shows decisively the practical, humane superiority of what Strauss calls "the first wave" of modernity, whose supreme political expression is the representative democracy structured by the American Constitution. Proven conclusively inferior, on the other hand, are the politics generated by the "second wave"—of Rousseau and German idealism, culminating in Marx and Marxism, and by the "third wave," of Nietzsche and Heidegger. Strauss's ancient liberalism finds important points of kinship with the modern liberalism based on Locke and Montesquieu.

In the first place, the essentially dissident character of classical liberal philosophy finds harbor in the fact that modern "liberals regard as sacred the right of everyone, however humble, odd, or inar-

ticulate, to criticize the government, including the man at the top."
In the second place, "with the increasing abundance" produced by
the liberation of competitive acquisitiveness, "it became increasingly possible to admit the element of hypocrisy which had entered
into the traditional notion of aristocracy," and, from the classical liberal viewpoint, it became "increasingly easy" to argue "practically or politically" that "all men have the same natural rights,
provided one uses this rule of thumb as the major premise for
reaching the conclusion that everyone should be given the same
opportunity as everyone else: natural inequality has its rightful
place in the use, nonuse, or abuse of opportunity" (LAM, Pref.
and 21).

Most important of all, Strauss stresses, is the fact that modern
liberal-democratic political life is capable in practice of surmount-
ing the low moral ceiling of its theoretical provenance. Most obviously in the American Founding period, and then in the careers
of Lincoln and Churchill, among others, liberal constitutionalism, at least when it is embattled, has shown that it can produce
statesmanship worthy of Plutarch. This is not simply accidental, or
against the grain of modern liberal republicanism. Strauss limns
the *Federalist*'s argument that representative government, when
based on an "electorate [that] is not depraved," has a "fair chance"
of electing delegates "who possess most wisdom to discern, and
most virtue to pursue, the common good" (quoting *Fed.* #57). It
is fair to say that the most massive legacy of Strauss as a university teacher has been the legion of scholars and teachers he has
spawned who have devoted their writings and their own teaching
to a renewal of critical reverence for the high moral and intellectual achievements of American democratic statesmanship, citizenship, and political thought. The polestar of this movement has
been Strauss's declaration that "the theoretical crisis" of modernity "does not *necessarily* lead to a practical crisis," "above all" because "liberal democracy, in contradistinction to communism and
fascism, derives powerful support from a way of thinking which
cannot be called modern at all: the premodern thought of our
western tradition" (TWM, 98—note that Strauss's term "premodern" encompasses both biblical and classical). Strauss concluded

his Introduction to the textbook he coedited with the emphatic reminder that "the authors of the *Federalist Papers* signed themselves 'Publius': republicanism points back to classical antiquity and therefore also to classical political philosophy" (HPP, 5). More precisely: "there is a direct connection between the [classic] notion of the mixed regime and modern republicanism" (LAM, 15–16).

Still: "lest this be misunderstood, one must immediately stress the important differences." More specifically, "the spring of this [modern republican] regime was held to be the desire of each to improve his material conditions. Accordingly the commercial and industrial elite, rather than the landed gentry, predominated." The intention of the *Federalist,* Strauss observes, is that the place held in the classical mixed regime by the liberally educated gentlemen is to be taken by "the learned professions," i.e., chiefly the lawyers. It is to those who are "most" virtuous "among" *these* that the *Federalist* looks for moral elevation of the regime. And Strauss endorses Burke's judgment: while the Law is a "science which does more to quicken and invigorate the understanding, than all the other kinds of learning put together," it is unfortunately the case that the Law is "not apt" to "open and to liberalize the mind" (LAM, 15–17).

In fanning the embers, within modern liberal democracy, of the older republican citizenship and statecraft Strauss does not, however, permit himself or encourage in others a nostalgic wish or hope for some kind of reconstruction of the ancient polis. This is what most obviously sets Strauss apart from communitarian and Heideggerian evokers of the Periclean "*vita activa*" and "public space," as well as from contemporaries who criticize "rights talk"; this is what most sharply distinguishes Strauss's politics from the politics of romanticism as well as the politics of Machiavelli, Rousseau, Marx, and Nietzsche—to mention only the most eloquent of the modern philosophic revolutionaries of the Right and of the Left. Strauss's long study of Aristophanes and Thucydides, and especially of the latter's dissection of all that is implied in the immoderation of Pericles' Funeral Oration, leaves Strauss—like those two great authors—unable to celebrate the splendors of imperialistic, growth-oriented Periclean democracy. Strauss's study of Thucydides and Aristophanes confirms his Platonic preference

for the older, quieter, more moderate Athens that Pericles deliberately (if unavoidably) had to destroy. Strauss is too thorough a student and admirer of the polis not to appreciate keenly the dangers
of attempts to transplant or to recreate somehow the polis within
modern conditions.

> We cannot reasonably expect that a fresh understanding of clas-
> sical political philosophy will supply us with recipes for today's
> use. For the relative success of modern political philosophy has
> brought into being a kind of society wholly unknown to the
> classics, a kind of society to which the classical principles as
> stated and elaborated by the classics are not immediately ap-
> plicable. Only we living today can possibly find a solution to the
> problems of today. But an adequate understanding of the prin-
> ciples as elaborated by the classics may be the indispensable
> starting point for an adequate analysis, to be achieved by us, of
> present-day society in its peculiar character, and for the wise ap-
> plication, to be achieved by us, of these principles to our tasks.
> (CM, 11)

Partly as a consequence, Strauss is not prone, as are more radical or "progressive" critics of liberalism, to speak contemptuously
of the "bourgeoisie," or to spurn with ingratitude the unprecedented extent of compassion, social welfare, and respect for individual freedom in diversity that has been brought about in and by
modern liberal democracy partnered with commerce or the free
market. Strauss saw more clearly than anyone the disharmony in
the American tradition, between an older, nobler, but less influential classical as well as biblical heritage, and a new, ever more triumphant, permissive, and individualistic order. But precisely for
this reason he saw more clearly the distinctive virtues and vices of
each component of this uneasy combination.

The combination is more and more threatened in our time by
the lamentable tendency of liberal democratic tolerance to degenerate, first into the easygoing belief that all points of view are equal
(hence none really worth or really capable of being defended with
passionate argument, deep analysis, or stalwart defense), and then
into the strident belief that anyone who does argue for the superi-

ority of a distinctive moral outlook, way of life, or human type is somehow "elitist" or antidemocratic—and thus immoral. This is the most recent version of the syndrome that Tocqueville diagnosed, in an earlier manifestation, as the new, soft "tyranny of the majority" to which modern democracy is prone: a subtle, unorganized, but all-pervasive pressure for egalitarian conformity arising from the psychologically chastened and intimidated individual's incapacity to resist the moral authority of mass "public opinion." In its most sublime expression, equality promises to every individual the opportunity to ascend to a just rank in the natural hierarchy of talents and attainments, of virtue and wisdom; but especially under the poisonous influence of the leveling moralism that disguises itself as "relativism," equality all too easily degrades itself. The problem is not alleviated by the thoughtlessly moralistic lurch away from relativism; for contemporary democratic moralism in its overt form tends to overstress the virtues of a rather flaccid sociability:

> there exists a very dangerous tendency to identify the good man with the good sport, the cooperative fellow, the "regular guy," i.e., an overemphasis on a certain part of social virtue and a corresponding neglect of those virtues which mature, if they do not flourish, in privacy, not to say in solitude: by educating people to cooperate with each other in a friendly spirit, one does not yet educate nonconformists, people who are prepared to stand alone, to fight alone, "rugged individualists." Democracy has not yet found a defense against the creeping conformism and the ever-increasing invasion of privacy which it fosters. . . . Now to the extent to which democracy is aware of these dangers, to the same extent it sees itself compelled to think of elevating its level and its possibilities by a return to the classics' notion of education. (WIPP, 38)

For Strauss, a relative strength of the politics flowing from the first wave of modernity was its "eminently sober" recognition of its "low but solid" foundations (using a Churchillian expression of which Strauss was fond—NRH, 247). The question classical republicanism impels is, whether such foundations are sufficient, or whether they do not decisively rely on the supplement of a spiritual sustenance derived from what are ever more rapidly disappearing vestiges of an older religious and classical liberal education. Modern liberal republicanism instantiates modern philosophy, which, "by causing the purpose of the philosophers, or more generally the purpose which essentially transcends society, to collapse into the purpose of the non-philosophers," thereby "causes the purpose of the gentlemen to collapse into the purpose of the nongentlemen." With the passage of years, "the understanding of virtue as choiceworthy for its own sake gave way to an instrumental understanding of virtue"; "virtue took on a narrow meaning, with the final result that the word 'virtue' fell into desuetude"—replaced by the "calculating transition from unenlightened to enlightened self-interest." Most significant of all, the Founders built their new republic on what the *Federalist* (#9, 57) understandably boasts of as a "great improvement" in the "science of politics," by which a marvelously well-wrought mechanism of checking and balancing institutions channels vigorously competitive self-interest. But this meant that "the devising of the right kind of institutions and their implementation came to be regarded as more important than the formation of character by liberal education" (LAM, 19–21).

Beyond the problem of the dwindling of the spiritual resources required for liberal republican energy and stability—a problem even on the premises of the moderns—there lies the even more profound human problem of cultural shallowness and growing spiritual emptiness. The enormity of this problem becomes manifest when we recognize its deep historical roots, reaching back to at least the late nineteenth century.

> Nietzsche once described the change which had been effected in the second half of the nineteenth century in continental Europe. The reading of the morning prayer had been replaced by the reading of the morning paper: not every day the same thing, the same reminder of man's absolute duty and exalted destiny, but every day something new with no reminder of duty and exalted destiny; specialization, knowing more and more

about less and less; the practical impossibility of concentration upon the very few essential things upon which man's wholeness entirely depends; the specialization compensated by sham universality, by the stimulation of all kinds of interests and curiosities without true passion; the danger of universal philistinism and creeping conformity. (RCPR, 31)

History proves that this is far from being a necessary entailment of democracy. Athenian democracy devoted its leisure to religious festivals where the citizenry were impelled to intense reflections on humanity's destiny in the whole as they wept at the complex contradictions of Sophocles and laughed at the deeply provocative absurdities of Aristophanes:

The means which Aristophanes employs in order to make us laugh include gossip or slander, obscenity, parody, and blasphemy. Through this ill-looking and ill-smelling mist we see free and sturdy rustics in their cups; good-natured; sizing up women, free or slave, as they size up cows and horses; in their best and gayest moments the fools of no one, be he god or wife or glorious captain, and yet less angry than amused at having been fooled by them ever so often; loving the country and its old and tested ways, despising the new-fangled and rootless which shoots up for a day in the city and among its boastful boosters; amazingly familiar with the beautiful so that they can enjoy every allusion to any of the many tragedies of Aeschylus, Sophocles, and Euripides; and amazingly experienced in the beautiful so that they will not stand for any parody which is not in its way as perfect as the original. Men of such birth and build are the audience of Aristophanes, or (which is the same for any non-contemptible poet) the best or authoritative part of his audience. The audience to which Aristophanes appeals or which he conjured is the best democracy as Aristotle has described it: the democracy whose backbone is the rural population. Aristophanes makes us see this audience at its freest and gayest, from its crude and vulgar periphery to its center of sublime delicacy; we do not see it equally well, although we sense it strongly, in its bonds and bounds. We see only half of it, apparently its lower half, in fact its higher. (RCPR, 107)

How does modern democracy appear, by this standard? Modern democracy fosters "mass culture," that is, "a culture which can be appropriated by the meanest capacities without any intellectual and moral effort whatsoever." This culture is dominated by the superficial "relaxation" or "entertainment" of hard-working "technicians" exercising "high-grade but strictly speaking unprincipled efficiency." "Thus we understand most easily what liberal education means here and now. Liberal education is the counterpoison to mass culture, to its inherent tendency to produce nothing but 'specialists without spirit or vision and voluptuaries without heart' [quoting Weber's conclusion to his *Protestant Ethic and the Spirit of Capitalism*]. Liberal education is the ladder by which we try to ascend from mass democracy to democracy as originally meant" (LAM, 5).

This means, however, that for us today, liberal education has unavoidably a different substance and purpose from what it had originally. The depleted and even desperate condition of this enterprise nowadays is the most widely and even deeply if dimly felt symptom of the failure of the first wave of the modern project to obviate the need for transcendent religious meaning. This profound failure explains the emergence of the second, and then the third, waves of modernity. These great movements of revolt against original modern rationalism strove, in what became fanatic failure, to implement a secular, radically modern or postmodern, high culture of exalted man-made humanity or superhumanity—first on a democratic footing (Rousseau to Marx) and then on an aristocratic (Nietzsche). It is the collapse of these "grandiose failures" that has ushered in "the crisis of our time," a crisis whose most obvious symptom is "that the difference between intellectuals and philosophers" becomes "blurred and finally disappears." "The crisis of modern natural right or of modern political philosophy could become a crisis of philosophy as such only because in the modern centuries philosophy as such had become thoroughly politicized. Originally, philosophy had been a pure source of humane inspiration and aspiration. Since the seventeenth century, philosophy has become a weapon, and hence an instrument" (NRH, 34).

SOME TENTATIVE LESSONS FOR CONTEMPORARY CIVIC LIFE

The massive primary civic lesson that follows from all this would appear to be threefold. To begin with, the rebirth of classical republican theory restores civic statesmanship to its princely throne as the highest subphilosophic human calling. And Strauss's teaching instills a tempered appreciation for the nobility of the political life within liberal democracy as the best regime possible in our epoch, in full awareness of this democracy's and that epoch's intensifying spiritual and civic conundrums. Strauss's thought carries an implicit as well as explicit severe rebuke of those thoughtlessly egalitarian historians and social scientists who debunk, rather than make more intelligible and vivid, the greatness of statesmen. Strauss deplores and opposes the prevalent scholarly tendency to belittle or to ignore political history for the sake of subpolitical "social" history—to reduce the debates and deeds of active citizens and their leaders to merely "ideological" contests masking supposedly deeper economic or "social" forces. He argues that these fashionable scholarly and teaching trends not only undermine the already precarious respect for political debate and public spirit, but also falsify the empirical reality of man as the political animal (WIPP, 27–28; LAM, 213–19).

At the same time, Strauss provides an immunization against—precisely by arousing a deep sympathy for the original motivations of—the terrible delusions that inspire the political fanaticism of the contemporary Left and Right, in their desperate attempts to replace liberal democracy with more elevated and radical versions of the great modern project, or in their hopeless attempts to bring about a political return to a lost preliberal and pious order.

By the same token, Strauss argues that we ought neither to expect nor to hope for an "end of history triumph" of American or of any other form of liberal democracy (see above all Strauss's great published debate with the Hegelian Alexandre Kojève, in OT).

Nothing in Strauss suggests that it is unreasonable to suppose that America and its liberal democracy will exercise planetary predominance or even hegemony for the foreseeable future. But it is unreasonable, given Strauss's analysis, to expect that the human spirit will not rise up in unforeseeable forms of longing and rebellion against the spiritual deformations imposed by and attendant upon this regime's predominance or hegemony. The yearning for transcendent purpose, and, most likely, the return to or recrudescence of some form of preliberal religiosity, will—if Strauss is right—remain permanent impulses bursting forth unpredictably from generation to generation. Nor is it likely that we will ever, so long as modernity prevails, see the end of various sorts of desperate nihilisms, that find perverse exaltation in dying to destroy that "evil" for which they cannot devise a viable replacement.

Those of civic ambition who are influenced by Strauss's reflections will presumably not await passively these grave threats to our liberal democracy. They will try to awaken others to their likelihood, in part by raising awareness of the controversial character of the deepest moral and religious foundations of liberal democracy. To possess this awareness is to recognize the fragility at the heart of our regime and to become all the more aware of the need for thoughtful action not only to defend modern liberalism but to shore it up—in part by supplementing it with ancient liberalism, in part by learning from ancient liberalism to elucidate moral potentials still present in contemporary liberalism that are in danger of extinction, through being forgotten or scorned. Not the least of what ancient liberalism teaches us is the fact that "religious diversity is the obstacle par excellence to conformism in this country" (LAM, 270).

STRAUSS'S "CONSERVATISM"

This implies that for most practical purposes Strauss's influence inclines toward the conservative part of the present-day spectrum (see Blitz, 1999). Classical political philosophy "cannot be simply conservative since it is guided by the awareness that all men seek by nature, not the ancestral or traditional, but the good."

Besides, "the conservatism of our age is identical with what was originally [modern] liberalism, more or less modified by changes in the direction of present-day liberalism." Yet as such, Strauss was apt to think, contemporary "conservatism" puts healthy brakes on contemporary liberalism, which is more infected by the visionary delusions of the second and third waves of modernity. "Liberals" (using the term now in the more narrow current sense), tend to agree with "Communism as regards the ultimate goal," which "may be said to be" the "universal and homogeneous state." "Pragmatic" liberals would be "satisfied with a federation of all now existing or soon emerging states, with a truly universal and greatly strengthened United Nations."

Conservatives tend to be soberly dubious about this trajectory. This is not because conservatives are still (as they tended to be in the nineteenth century) simply nationalistic, let alone imperial: "there is no reason whatever," Strauss opined, "why they should be opposed to a United Free Europe, for instance. Yet they are likely to understand such units differently from the liberals. An outstanding European conservative [De Gaulle] has spoken of *l'Europe des patries.*" In other words, "conservatives look with greater sympathy than liberals on the particular or particularist and the heterogeneous; at least they are more willing than liberals to respect and perpetuate a more fundamental diversity." Strauss means, in the first place, a political diversity, rooted in the nations, with their distinct and healthily competing traditions; but more fundamentally he means religious diversity, within as well as among nations: "religion rather than science is the bulwark of genuine diversity"; "it seems that only a qualifiedly secularist, that is, a qualifiedly religious, state which respects equally religious and nonreligious people can be counted upon to contain within itself the remedy against the ill of conformism" (LAM, Pref. and 265, 270; see also Plattner, 2002).

Behind this is a comprehensive conservative critique for which Strauss expresses his qualified respect, and which he summarizes as follows: today's "politically relevant cosmopolitanism" tends to be accompanied by a "decay of the spirit, of taste, of the mind," because it is rooted in or strongly prone to "the belief that human life as such, i.e., independently of the kind of life one leads, is an absolute good." Accordingly it embraces and even promotes a peculiar "humanitarianism" that goes hand in hand with "an overriding concern with pleasure and unwillingness or inability to dedicate one's life to ideals." "It does not leave room for reverence, the matrix of human nobility": for "reverence is primarily, i.e., for most men at all times and for all men most of the time, reverence for one's heritage, for tradition." And "traditions are essentially particularistic," or "akin to nationalism rather than to cosmopolitanism" (WIPP, 236–38).

Strauss parts company with this line of thought inasmuch as he is convinced by the classics that the "natural political community is, not the nation, but the city." "A city is a community commensurate with man's natural powers of firsthand or direct knowledge." It is a community "in which a mature man can find his bearings through his known observation, without having to rely habitually on indirect information in matters of vital importance." For "direct knowledge of men can safely be replaced by indirect knowledge only so far as the individuals who make up the political multitude are uniform or 'mass-men.'" Besides, "only a society small enough to permit mutual trust is small enough to permit mutual responsibility or supervision—the supervision of actions or manners which is indispensable for a society concerned with the perfection of its members." Just as "man's natural power of first hand knowledge, so his power of love or of active concern, is by nature limited" (WIPP, 237; NRH, 131).

"The nation would thus appear," Strauss concludes in demurral from modern conservatives, as an unsatisfactory "half-way house between the polis and the cosmopolis." The deep truth groped toward but not grasped adequately by contemporary conservatism, in its appreciation of national political diversity, is the "substantive principle" of classical political philosophy: "every political society that ever has been or ever will be rests on a particular fundamental opinion which cannot be replaced by knowledge and hence is of necessity a particular or particularistic society" (WIPP, 238; LAM, Pref.).

But this means that we must do justice to the truth groped

toward but not grasped adequately by contemporary cosmopolitanism. Each and every particular society, and each city most of all, "in one way or another qualifies the principle of merit, i.e., the principle par excellence of justice, by the wholly unconnected principle of indigenousness." In addition, "citizen-morality suffers from an inevitable self-contradiction." It "asserts that different rules of conduct apply in war than in peace, but it cannot help regarding at least some relevant rules, which are said to apply in peace only, as universally valid." "To avoid this self-contradiction," the city "must transform itself into the 'world-state.'" Yet this means a world entirely ruled by someone or some very few. And "no human being and no group of human beings can rule the whole world justly." Therefore, "what is divined in speaking of the 'world-state' as an all-comprehensive human society subject to one human government is in truth the cosmos ruled by God, which is then the only true city, or the city that is simply according to nature." Men are full "citizens of this city," "only if they are wise; their obedience to the law which orders the natural city, to the natural law, is the same thing as prudence." "This solution to the problem of justice obviously transcends the limits of political life" (NRH, 149–51).

SOME IMPLICATIONS FOR FOREIGN POLICY

In practical terms, this would imply, as regards foreign policy, a classical republican recognition of the permanence of international conflict—together with, and in some measure the basis of, international cooperation. I say "classical republican" because this would be a recognition of the permanence of competition among political societies, due not simply to a Hobbesian or Nietzschean competition for power, or even to the diversification of humanity into warring peoples by "history," but even more to humanity's ever present, terrible potential for tyrannic perversion of its natural political passions—which, to become healthy and ennobled, are so much in need of moral education. Against both liberal and Communist idealism Strauss protested that "no bloody or unbloody change of society can eradicate the evil in man" (CM, 5). At the deepest level, however, the classical republican sees the inextirpable root of international conflict in the political insolubility of the problem of justice. "Human beings will never create a society which is free of contradictions" (LAM, 230). If Socratic utopianism is right, then the impossibility in principle of a society that is not in some important way morally partial (blinded) entails a perpetually competing, and sometimes mortally competing, diversity of legitimate aspirations to the just society.

A citizen of our liberal democracies who was penetrated by this awareness[2] would presumably attempt to cultivate in foreign policy a liberal outlook that, in a spirit ready to learn and to argue, holds open the door to dialogue with decent and thoughtful critics emerging from alien and especially more traditional sorts of social and religious outlooks. The fact that Strauss's own education received its most important impulse from his intense study of philosophers within the world of Islam sets a pregnant example.

But such a citizen would also feel keenly the need to be prepared to struggle and to fight in defense of liberal democracy. From the classical republican perspective, this sad necessity and truth would appear to be not entirely without compensations. Resolute and active defense of liberal democracy, shoulder to shoulder with energetic and thoughtfully critical allies, can be a source of renewal of high purpose, of exemplary civic spirit and thoughtful reflection, of citizen engagement and even participation. At the same time, the global foreign policy of an aroused superpower imposes an invigorating challenge on democratic leadership (and on that leadership's electorate). A major part of this challenge involves resisting the temptations to quasi-imperial domination and close-minded self-satisfaction, or self-righteousness. All this implies that even foreign and defense policy needs to be viewed in terms not only of defense, and of benefit to others, but also—if only secondarily—in terms of the moral effects on domestic political life, on the virtues of the citizenry.

Preeminent among those virtues is moderation. Strauss often sums up what distinguishes his Socratic or classical liberalism and republicanism from modern liberalism and republicanism in "the old saying that wisdom cannot be separated from moderation." "Moderation will protect us against the twin dangers of visionary expectations from politics and unmanly contempt for politics" (LAM, 24). Strauss insists that the mating of moderation with wisdom entails among other things that "wisdom requires unhesitating loyalty to a decent constitution and even to the cause of constitutionalism." But this is so far from preventing, that it requires, constructive criticism. "We are not permitted to be flatterers of democracy precisely because we are friends and allies of democracy." Yet "while we are not permitted to remain silent on the dangers to which democracy exposes itself as well as human excellence, we cannot forget the obvious fact that by giving freedom to all, democracy also gives freedom to those who care for human excellence." It is not enough to enjoy this freedom by "cultivating our garden," unless at the same time we see our gardening as also "setting up outposts which may come to be regarded by many citizens as salutary to the republic and as deserving of giving to it its tone." "It is in this way that the liberally educated may again receive a hearing even in the market place" (LAM, 24). And this, we may conclude, is the heart of Strauss's own politics, in the narrow sense of the word.

4 : Strauss's Legacy in Political Science

Strauss expresses his admiration for the "intrepidity of thought," the "grandeur of vision," the "graceful subtlety of speech," and the profound political astuteness as well as "public spirit" that characterize the philosophic originators of the great modern project. He readily acknowledges the magnitude of the project's world-historical achievements. But he "inclines" to the judgment that modernity, taken as a whole in all its unfolding richness, represents an estrangement from "erotic" human nature as revealed or confirmed by Socratic dialectics; in this light, it is not so surprising that the project has culminated in a spiritual "crisis" of humanity as such. Strauss's complex diagnosis of the roots or causes points out a potential path, however, through the crisis: the "tentative or experimental" revival of Socratic political philosophy—and our own original application, to our unprecedented form of society, of the Aristotelian political science and liberal education that was the fullest civic expression of Socratic philosophy.[1]

AN ARISTOTELIAN SCIENCE OF MODERN POLITICS: THE THEORETICAL FRAMEWORK

What may be called Strauss's "tentative or experimental" "philosophy of social science" begins from the Socratic premise that a responsible science of politics should be concerned to promote political health and a robust civic life, while diagnosing and seeking remedies for political pathology. From this premise it follows that political *philosophy* must guide, rather than being merely one "field" within, sound political *science*. For it is political philosophy that pursues and wrestles with the essential guiding questions: what is civic health? what is justice or the common good? what is human flourishing?

Yet this leading role of political philosophy can easily be the source of grave misconception. In the classical view, with which we are "experimenting," political philosophy pilots political science in a most delicate and ambiguous sense. If political philosophy, and the political science guided by political philosophy, are to avoid disastrous missteps from the very outset, they must take their bearings by listening with docility to, and then questioning, clarifying, and critically deepening (and thus defending and assisting) the "political *wisdom*" or the "civic *art*" of respected and experienced citizens and statesmen.[2] For reflective "common sense" has knowledge, if imperfect knowledge, of sound guiding principles of civic action; and this *practical* knowledge possessed by the active and engaged citizen or statesman is *prior* to and even in a crucial sense *independent* of theoretical science or philosophy. Strauss goes so far as to declare that "the sphere governed by prudence" is "in principle self-sufficient." He immediately concedes, however, that in fact this sphere is ceaselessly breached by perplexing assaults from "false doctrines" that claim to provide the answers to those questions that are indeed "the most important questions"—questions about the character of justice and about humanity's situation and fate within the whole. The reason why practical wisdom is constantly being perplexed by these answers offered from "outside," or from suprapolitical "authorities," is that the fundamental questions being answered in this way "are not stated, let alone answered, with sufficient clarity by practical wisdom itself." The prudent citizens and statesmen need help in disposing of these questions, and the "outside" challenges that provoke them; and that is why their otherwise self-sufficient "practical wisdom" is dependent, "*de facto*," though not "*de jure*," on political philosophy as "practical *science*."[3]

Aristotelian political science is then necessary first and foremost as the theoretical defender of untheoretical and even to some extent unreflective practical wisdom—against hostile or demeaning and confusing theoretical challengers. Secondarily, however, there is need and room for a comprehensive study of political praxis by a "political science" that takes its bearing from Aristotle's *Politics* and that thus aims to clarify and deepen, thus assisting, the citizen's and statesman's practical wisdom. Political philosophy per se, and then, in addition, the science of politics that is guided by political philosophy, combine to enlighten prudence. But they do so, not chiefly by looking at politics from a different and presumed superior perspective, but rather by striving as much as possible to adopt the *same* perspective as the active statesmen—only inevitably seeing *further,* in the sense both of looking more comprehensively and of looking more deeply.[4]

"The Pit beneath the Natural Cave"

Yet in our time, this primarily defensive, and secondarily enlightening, vocation—this need for political philosophy to protect, while also enlarging the autonomy of, the statesman's prudential wisdom—takes on a new complexity unknown to the classics. For the cultural revolution effected first by "pseudo-philosophy," and then by modern political philosophy, in an understandable if excessive reaction against the former's victory, has made it look as if theory must be the *source,* and not only the helpful defensive and supplemental guide, of the practical norms that govern political action. As a result, common sense has for a number of centuries been overawed and pervasively contaminated—in the classical view—by a parade of dialectically competing, pseudo-philosophic and philosophic doctrines that have usurped the prerogative of dictating to prudence its ends. This perverse (i.e., unnatural and, strictly speaking, accidental) process has left prudence and praxis in a mutilated condition—which afflicts everyone in the West in some degree. It is this pervasive disease of practical reasoning which, from the classical perspective, gives prima facie evidence for, and even some justification of, the historicist contention as to the historical mutability of prudence and hence of praxis. This much is certain: the successive failure of each and all of these theoretical usurpers (various theories of "natural law," the "state of nature" or the "original position" and the "social contract," the "categorical imperative," the "philosophy of history," "positivism," "utilitarianism," "Marxism," "socialism," "existentialism," "libertarianism," "postmodernism," etc., etc.) has left common sense, in our time, sliding into still more self-alienating enthrallment to the "scientific study of politics": originally as "behavioralism," which sought to combine the tools of modern statistics and modern psychology to explain and predict observable, quantifiable political action or "behavior"; and more recently as "rational choice," which takes its inspiration from mathematized economics, including game theory, with its assumption of "utility maximization" as the key to human behavior.[5]

This last desperate move is not without a certain plausibility, since mathematical science is the sole part of modern rationalism that has not experienced what appears to be disgracefully deflating failure. Strauss demurs, nonetheless; he warns that "social science" will go ever more widely astray insofar as it looks to modern mathematical science as something more than a subordinate, if (within its proper bounds) marvelously effective, tool.[6] Far be it from those who take their inspiration from Plato to show disrespect for the revelatory truth-giving of mathematics: "God geometrizes." Yet, as one of modernity's greatest theoretical mathematicians teaches, however divine may be "the spirit of geometry," it must bow to the still more divine "spirit of finesse." This latter spirit is more akin to the "civic art" than is the "spirit of geometry" or of mathematics. In his essay, "Social Science and Humanism," Strauss elaborates on Pascal's famous aphoristic dichotomy as follows: "The scientific spirit is characterized by detachment and by the forcefulness which stems from simplicity or simplification. The spirit of finesse is characterized by attachment or love and by breadth. The principles to which the scientific spirit defers are alien to common sense. The principles with which the spirit of finesse has to do are within common sense, yet they are barely visible; they are felt rather than seen. They are not available in such a way that we could make them the premises of our reasoning. The spirit of finesse is active, not in reasoning, but rather in grasping in one view unanalyzed wholes in their distinctive characters" (RCPR, 3).

The modern mathematical-scientific spirit and its method (even or especially when it is most self-consciously dependent, for its "criteria of relevance," on modern "normative theory") is constitutionally incapable of doing full justice to what is distinctively human. Modern scientific method is unavoidably reductionist. It takes its bearings by the premise, that, "in order to understand a whole, one must analyze or resolve it into its elements, one must study the elements by themselves, and then one must reconstruct the whole or recompose it by starting from the elements." But the question is: can the relevant political wholes—countries, regimes, institutions, competing civic and moral codes or principles of life, political parties and movements, even individual citizens—be thus reduced to their elements without being distorted in their true being? And in any case, the "reconstruction requires that the whole be sufficiently grasped in advance, prior to the analysis." For "if the primary grasp lacks definiteness and breadth, both the analysis and the synthesis will be guided by a distorted view of the whole, by a figment of a poor imagination rather than by the thing in its fullness." In addition, "the elements at which the analysis arrives will be at best only *some* of the elements." Now the grave problem is, that "the whole as primarily known is an object of common sense; but it is of the essence of the scientific spirit, at least as this spirit shows itself within the social sciences, to be distrustful of common sense or even to discard it altogether" (RCPR, 4).

The consequence is, that mathematically inspired social science may indeed, if it is astutely attentive to the commonsense understanding, shed important light on the *lower* aspects of human existence; but it does so at the price of running the risk of obscuring or distorting the higher aspects.[7] Above all, mathematically dominated or guided political science has no eyes to see what is in fact *the* critical factor in all political "behavior": the human being's passionate concern with *to kalon*—with "the noble/beautiful," with self-respect, with dignity, as a rational and thus free being capable of dedication, devotion, and even sacrifice for the sake of causes perceived as just and as thereby partaking of transcendent or eternal value. What mathematically dominated political science misses, or is unable to see, is more important than what such science, properly and modestly employed, can illuminate. For "it is safer to try to understand the low in the light of the high than the high in the light of the low." This methodological principle follows from the observation of the following necessity: "in doing the latter one necessarily distorts the high" (Strauss means, one necessarily distorts the empirical phenomena, because the very meaning of the high, as it presents itself in our experience, is that it is *not* reducible to or explicable in terms of the low), "whereas in doing the former one does not deprive the low of the freedom to reveal itself as what it is" (since the high is so far from denying, that it rather strongly affirms, the independent existence and power of the low, even as it comes to sight in our experience—LAM, 225).

The Politeia *or "Regime"*

This passionate concern for what is high, for what has dignity, for *to kalon*—this spiritual core of the human as the political animal—is the deepest source of the contest that keeps politics ceaselessly in motion. For, as we learn vividly in Book Three of Aristotle's *Politics,* the moral virtues, distilled from unmutilated common sense as the core of true nobility, manifest themselves politically in forms distorted by passions—evil, crass, and sublime. The claim to uphold and to advance some notion of justice, some notion of righteousness, fairness, and the common good, is always at the heart of political action; but this claim is always put forth, justice is always in practice defined, in a partisan and biased spirit. Political life is riven by competition among adherents of conflicting "regimes" (*politeiai*)—democracy, oligarchy, aristocracy, monarchy, theocracy, and so forth—in their various versions and even mixtures. What is at stake becomes fully evident only when one recognizes, with Aristotle, that each regime aims to advance, and as it gains victory imposes, a specific moral ranking of the various human types and their excellences (the priests, the warriors, the poor majority of proletarians, the landed gentry, the yeoman farmers, the merchants, the businessmen, etc., etc.). The regime's distinctive ranking is clearly expressed by the degree of civic authority, or share in rule, assigned by that regime to each human class or type. Every such ranking, by each regime, lays a claim to justice: each defining, predominant part or class claims that it is *entitled* to rule; and this claim implies a more or less severe moral condemnation of contrasting and competing regimes and their rankings and claims to entitlement.

In every society, the regime, as the outcome of the struggle over which human type or types will be morally preponderant, shapes the "way of life" more than any other formative factor except for human nature itself. The contest among competing aspirants to define the regime is then the supremely important contest in human existence; and a political science worthy of the name must keep this most fundamental political fact squarely in view.[8] One may make the same point by declaring that the only genuine social science is the science of regimes or political science (and its subordinates: *political* economy, *political* psychology, *political* history, etc.). All social sciences that, in our time, claim autonomy from political science fundamentally misunderstand the nature of human society. They remain enthralled to the basic "spirit of our time." They have been led astray by the distortions that are the outcome of the modern break with classical political philosophy.

A self-consciously Aristotelian political science will study the contest among the regimes in the light of an inquiry into the "best regime simply"—the regime that would be dedicated to the maximum possible human fulfillment. But such a political science will be fully aware that, while the "best regime" must be articulated as a standard, for that very reason it cannot be regarded as a practical goal. In fact, the full articulation of the best regime reveals that very regime to be itself riven by insoluble tensions—above all, between the civic or moral virtues and the (ultimately higher) philosophic virtues. These tensions clarify the limitations on all political life, and make precise the reasons for the political intractability of human nature.[9] By the same token, the effort to articulate the best regime renders stark the fact that none of the actual parties to the fundamental dispute among the regimes—none of the various forms of democracy, oligarchy, monarchy, tyranny, theocracy, etc. (and mixtures thereof)—stand for more than a partial and dimly perceived version of justice and the good life. Nonetheless, each is defined above all by its dedication to some imperfect conception of the just and good life. The political scientist's proper role in the conflict among regimes and over the regime is neither that of a partisan, nor that of a neutral, "scientific" observer engaging in merely "comparative" politics. The political scientist's proper role is that of an unofficial umpire or judge (WIPP, 80–81).

In order to fulfill this role, political science in the proper sense seeks to attain a sympathetic understanding of the competing regimes, such as allows the articulation of an argumentative dialogue among their principles and practices in the light of the standard set by the best regime simply. Through such a dialogue, each regime's moral weaknesses may be examined for possible reform, and its moral strengths spotlighted for enhancement and imitation. "Social science cannot then rest satisfied with the overall objectives of whole societies as they are for the most part understood in social life. Social science must clarify those objectives, ferret out their self-contradictions and halfheartedness, and strive for knowledge of the true overall objectives of whole societies" (RCPR, 6).The closest approach to such a political science emerging from or on the modern premises and as applied to modern liberal democracy may be said to be Tocqueville's *Democracy in America*.[10]

To follow in Tocqueville's path, regarding Tocquevillian political science as a kind of modern echo of Aristotelian political science, is to concede that for all or most purposes of immediate political analysis an Aristotelian outlook has many important things to learn from what Alexander Hamilton speaks of as the "great improvement" that the "science of government" has received in modernity. Whether we consider modern federalism, or modern representative institutions (including modern political parties), or the modern systems of checks and balances, centered on the modern idea of the separation of powers, we find "powerful means, by which the excellencies of republican government may be retained and its imperfections lessened or avoided" (*Federalist Papers,* no. 9). Nor is it only in the superior design of key governmental institutions and practices that our form of polity, and the political theorizing that spawned it, can claim to have improved markedly upon what we find in classical republican theory and practice: the abolition of slavery and the concomitant dignifying of free labor; the integration of women into citizenship and education; the vastly increased relief of the mass of the citizenry from poverty and ill health; the discoveries of the sciences and not least of the science of economics—all these signal major respects in which civic life has advanced under the tutelage of modern political philosophy. The enormous costs and the insoluble dilemmas that are attendant upon and inseparable from these advances do not negate the fact that they are advances that would be recognized as such by Aristotle.

Yet we must go further. For we have been speaking as if the advances of modern theory and practice are to be understood as supplements to, or are to be integrated into, an essentially Aristotelian political science and understanding. We have been speaking as if we could presume or assume that Aristotle's teaching on politics is the true teaching. But we are not in a position to make so momentous an assumption. In other words, we have to resist the temptation to lose sight of the "tentative or experimental" character of Strauss's whole proposal. In "experimenting" with the possibility that Aristotle can supply us with the decisive guidance for comprehending political life we must remain open to, and must even seriously entertain, the possibility that we will discover that, on the contrary, the wisdom we doubtless can and need to recover from Aristotle must in the final analysis be integrated into the truer teachings of one or another version of modern political philosophy (e.g., Tocqueville)—or even into the late-modern philosophic teaching that demands the abandonment of political philosophy as impossible and unnecessary. Yet, to repeat, such an outcome would not by any means altogether cancel out the wisdom that is available to us, and in need of retrieval, from Aristotelian political science.

At the heart of that wisdom is the focus on the regime as the supreme political phenomenon, as the core of a society's self-definition and hence its very existence as the distinct society that it is. Aristotle further teaches that the gravest internal dangers for any particular regime are almost always those least noted by its partisans, because those dangers are inherent in the unchecked supremacy of the regime's own favorite and dominant moral spirit —and because, as a consequence, those who dare to prescribe the needed antidotes will almost inevitably be suspected of being "anti-regime" (Aristotle *Politics* Bk. 5, chap. 9, end). Now since the political scientist, as a loyal citizen, will exert his chastising scientific efforts first and foremost on his own regime, in its competing strands and in controversy with its most serious international and historical competitors, this means that the genuine political scientist will almost inevitably incur moral opprobrium in his own community. One is tempted to say that some degree of such opprobrium is the brand of honor signaling the authentic, as opposed to the sophistic, political scientist.

In modern democracy, the courageously loyal political scientist will, imitating Tocqueville, limn the democratic dangers to democracy by reminding of aristocracy's and monarchy's contrasting moral and spiritual and civic strengths. He will not allow it to be forgotten that democracy "is meant to be an aristocracy which has broadened into a universal aristocracy"; that "liberal education is the ladder by which we try to ascend from mass democracy to democracy as originally meant." He will endure, even as a badge of pride, the odious epithet "elitist" that attends the democratic political scientist who, if he is the genuine article, relentlessly points, in a reformist spirit, to the dangers inherent in the unchecked advance of the treasured moral principles of equality and individual liberty and popular sovereignty and economic "growth": "the dangers inherent in liberal democracy will be set forth squarely"; "the sensitivity to these dangers will be sharpened and, if need be, awakened." In Strauss's lapidary words, "we are not permitted to be flatterers of democracy precisely because we are friends and allies of democracy."[11] This means that in the best case the political scientist's loyal love of his own country and people is in a sense transfigured by something that crowns his political science and may be called his "humanism":

> By reflecting on what it means to be a human being, one sharpens one's awareness of what is common to all human beings, if in different degrees, and of the goals toward which all human beings are directed by the fact that they are human beings. One

transcends the horizon of the mere citizen—of every kind of sectionalism—and becomes a citizen of the world. Humanism as awareness of man's distinctive character as well as of man's distinctive completion, purpose, or duty issues in humaneness: . . . a last and not merely last freedom from the degradation or hardening effected especially by conceit or pretense. . . . Yet, even if all were said that could be said and that cannot be said, humanism is not enough. Man, while being at least potentially a whole, is only a part of a larger whole. . . . That whole, or its origin, is either subhuman or superhuman. Man cannot be understood in his own light but only in the light of either the subhuman or the superhuman. . . . Mere humanism avoids this ultimate issue. . . . It is from this point of view that we can begin to understand again the original meaning of science, of which the contemporary meaning is only a modification: science as man's attempt to understand the whole to which he belongs . . . [from] the perspective of the citizen of the world, in the twofold meaning of "world": the whole human race and the all-embracing whole. (RCPR, 7–8)

AN ARISTOTELIAN SCIENCE OF MODERN POLITICS

The grounding expressions of neo-Aristotelian political science are necessarily polemical: in our epoch, common sense has first to be sprung free from the thought control exercised by the established intelligentsia of Left and Right. Leading the way in this guerilla war to liberate the imprisoned, especially those in the grip of positivistic social science, are Strauss's dissection of Max Weber's "nihilist" self-contradictions, and Storing's (1962: chap. 2) exposure of the debilitating incoherences in the Nobel laureate Herbert Simon's pseudoscientific theory of decision and management.[12] But, while this kind of foundational criticism has continued, expanding to meet new manifestations of the relativistic and historicist "scientific study" of politics,[13] there has been erected on these foundations a substantial literature exemplifying an alternative analysis, including the proper employment of the new quantitative tools modern mathematical science makes available.

Political Economy

A constructive sequel to Storing's critique of Herbert Simon is Rhoads's sympathetic analysis (1985) of "the economist's view of the world." This book delineates the moral as well as empirical strengths of micro-, welfare-, and benefit/cost-economic analyses, while showing precisely how those very strengths risk hypertrophic distortion of their subject matter if they do not defer to moral, cultural, and psychological categories made available in Strauss-led and Strauss-inspired explications of Plato, Rousseau, and Tocqueville.[14] In general, those penetrated by Strauss who have engaged with contemporary economic thinking have insisted on the need for continual reencounter with the texts of the philosophic founders of modern "political economy" (Hobbes, Locke, Montesquieu, Hume, Smith, Ferguson, etc., as well as the great debate between Hamilton and Jefferson soon after the American Founding). It is in those texts alone that one can find, and truly test the cogency of, justifications for the most basic (and controversial, nay, deeply problematic) normative and moral commitments uncritically and often unconsciously at work in contemporary economic science and theories of what is called "rational choice."[15] In this enterprise, and in the retrieval, from the ashen hands of conventional historicist scholarship, of the true but half-hidden positions of thinkers such as Locke, there is some overlap between Strauss-inspired and the most sophisticated Marx-inspired scholarship (cf. esp. SPPP, chap. 13 with Macpherson, 1962 and 1972).

The Political Psychology of Leadership and Citizenship

Robert Horwitz's searing critique of Harold Lasswell's Freudian-inspired science of leadership "personality" (Storing, 1962: chap. 4) has been carried forward, especially through criticisms of the application of scientific-psychological "personality" typologies to the American presidency. Truly empirical psychology of leadership, those influenced by Strauss contend, has to rise to the difficult challenge of evaluating the virtues and vices, the moral character, of leaders as leaders; for *character* is the true phenomenon underlying and generating the epiphenomena of "personality," and "style"—with which contemporary political psychology is excessively obsessed. An intimate familiarity with the vivid accounts of the moral and civic virtues provided by Aristotle, Cicero, and other great classical moral theorists, affords a richly concrete foundation for the critical estimation of leadership character. And acutely significant in this regard is painstaking analysis of the meaning and role played by the longing for eternity that expresses itself as the love of fame.[16]

Forbes's work (1985) has shown how the deployment of the Platonic regime-psychology adumbrated in the eighth book of Plato's *Republic* can provide the basis for a sound critical revision of the Frankfurt school's political personality studies and their implications. Forbes's later work on ethnic conflict (1997), testing systematically the famous "contact hypothesis" (roughly speaking, the hypothesis that increased familiar intermingling between ethnic groups promotes greater mutual acceptance) is exemplary of Strauss-inspired employment of quantitative methods, where appropriate, in the execution of a political psychology and sociology whose horizon is explicitly Montesquieuian in human breadth and moral depth.

The neo-Aristotelian approach subordinates, however, the study of quantifiable mass effects, opinion, and behavior to the scrutiny of writings, speeches, and recorded utterances, authored by citizens and civic leaders at various levels but especially at the highest. The working hypothesis is, that the conceptions shaping the evolution of a political society's way of life are most visibly in play where those with access to rule, or those seeking such access, articulate and fight over moral goals, principles, and priorities, in response to defining problems and crises that are the turning points of historical action. Accordingly, for the neo-Aristotelian political scientist, the "data" that are most important—the speeches and writings that most powerfully shape and thus explain the present order—are at least as likely to be found in the formative past of a regime or nation as in the present.

The Pathology of Tyranny

This paramountcy, as shaping causal forces, of struggles over the regime—of those struggles the actors themselves consider crucial—holds even in tyrannic regimes. Analysis guided by Strauss stresses, of course, the supreme importance of the need never to lose sight of the moral inferiority of tyranny, despite the partial and disquieting advantages that such rule may possess. But even tyrants, the classical analysts teach us, cannot escape the natural and overriding human need for moral justification. Classically inspired study of the inner workings of tyrannies focuses on the (often Byzantine) contests among aspirants to embody the regime's leading human qualities. These competitions take on a new, characteristic complexity in modernity, inasmuch as tyranny manifests itself in a new and unprecedented form: modern tyranny tends to be "ideological," that is, to understand itself as guided by some comprehensive, normative-scientific, quasi-philosophic analysis of the human situation. The struggle over the regime is therefore simultaneously a struggle over what is to be the orthodox interpretation of the justifying ideological theory. This ideological character of modern tyranny was exhibited most powerfully in Communism. Paradigmatic studies that show the footprint of Strauss are Baras's account (1975) of the crucial stages in Ulbricht's, and thereby East Germany's, career of self-definition; Rush's analyses (1958; 1965; 1974; 1993) of the evolution of the post-Stalinist Soviet and East European regimes, centering on the succession struggles in the leadership; and Fairbanks's exploration (1993; 1995a; 1995b; 1997) of the reasons for the decline, fall, and aftermath of the Soviet Union. The key failing of conventional Soviet studies, as seen from the perspective afforded by Strauss, is summed up thus by Fairbanks (1993: 50–51):

> It is impossible to understand the collapse of Soviet Communism without appreciating the role of ideas and convictions in history. . . . [T]he communist system was . . . destroyed, in large part because of the contradiction between ideals and reality. . . . One of the effects of our scholarship's depreciation of ideas and convictions was the expectation that, if there was to be re-

form in the Soviet Union, it would be made by "technocrats" or "pragmatists" such as industrial managers, not by people who were most closely identified with the alien or communist side of the regime, such as the ideological specialists within the Party apparatus, the closely related leadership of the international communist movement, and the political police. . . . It was thus a surprise to find the "secret police" intimately involved in the origins of *perestroika*. . . . It was also a surprise to find militant reformers within the ideological specialization of the Party apparatus. . . .

International Relations

Strauss-generated study of foreign policy and international relations (including international law) has been rooted in a revolution in Thucydidean interpretation, bringing out the close kinship between Thucydides and the Socratics. The predominant pre-Straussian notion of Thucydides among political theorists is expressed in Walzer's still-influential treatment, which dismisses Thucydides as representative of a "realism" whose "purpose" is to make moral "discourse about particular cases appear to be idle chatter."[17] Strauss and his followers have executed sustained exegesis to show that, on the contrary, Thucydides' central theme is an exploration, unrivaled in its depth and lack of sentimentality, of the true meaning and full force of justice among nations as that meaning and force actually emerge in political speech and action at its peak, in the conflict between the two greatest alternative forms of republican regime.[18] These new Thucydidean studies have exposed contemporary so-called realist and neorealist international theory as unrealistic in its failure to take into account how drastically foreign policy and international behavior varies with the varying regimes and their competing moral outlooks.[19]

As an antistrophe, we find a line of sympathetic but skeptical examinations of the strengths and weaknesses of modern philosophic, especially Kantian, international idealism—in practice as well as in theory.[20] Fukuyama, inspired by Strauss, but breaking with him, has made famous an updated version of the provocative "end of history" thesis that Strauss's dialogic antagonist, the Marxist-Hegelian Alexandre Kojève, set forth, especially in his great published debate with Strauss: the contention that the true (Hegelian) philosophic account explains the culminating, world-historical meaning of the fall of Soviet Communism and thus the fated dispensation of the centuries upon which we are entering.[21]

More recently, scholars indebted to Strauss have wrestled with the questions surrounding the post–Cold War attempts to limit national sovereignty in the name of "multilateralism" and new forms of confederal association.[22] What sets these studies apart from other such efforts (which lack the benefit of Strauss's guidance or provocation) is their insistence on reaching back into great historical moments and thinkers in order to retrieve crucial forgotten presuppositions of both sovereignty and its alternatives. Rabkin, in particular (1997, 1998a, 1998b, 2005), has manfully maintained that our leading contemporary authorities in and out of governments have lost sight of the deep benefits—for republican self-government as well as for national and international security—that were descried by, and gave such power to the arguments of, the modern political theorists of sovereignty.

THE AMERICAN REGIME AND CONSTITUTION

Not only the civic allegiance of Strauss himself and most of those he shaped, but in addition the towering significance of America in today's planetary culture, dictates putting the study of American politics at center stage. And the heart of American politics, in Strauss's view, is the Constitution and its evolution— viewed as the working out of the not altogether harmonizing basic principles enunciated in the Revolution (above all in the Declaration of Independence) and the subsequent Constitutional Founding. To discover the Constitution's full meaning as the basic law of the regime is to achieve clarity about the overarching moral goals, the way of life, the human types, that the Constitution fosters— and, conversely, those it discourages. The study of the Founding epoch is especially revealing in these regards. This is partly because, in examining any founding, we may observe the foundations in the act of being laid. But in the American case the Founding is uniquely revelatory, because the American Constitutional Founding was blessed with leaders—and leading opponents (among the Anti-Federalists)—of unusual wisdom and articulateness.[23] Not only do these men of action speak for themselves, but they point us with some explicitness to their philosophic teachers, above all (though by no means exclusively) Locke and Montesquieu.[24]

The Founding is of course not the end of the story. But the Founding sets the horizon within which move subsequent developments—even when they verge on "re-foundings" (the Jeffersonian and Jacksonian movements, the struggles over slavery and race; the response to the Great Depression, the Cold War). The Founding exhibits unsolved and even insoluble problems that keep the regime in troubled motion, and that surface at periods of great tension or struggle over the meaning of the regime.[25] The scientist of American government will continually miss the deep (and contestable) presuppositions and entailments of the system he is studying if he fails constantly to recur to a meticulous and meditative reflection on the writings and especially the debates of the Founding period, situating them in contrast with the great alternative philosophies of republicanism, ancient and modern.

This means, to be sure, that the neo-Aristotelian political scientist will soon become aware of a deep and half-hidden complexity in the nature of the regime under the conditions of modern political life—shaped as that life is, largely though not completely, by modern political theory. For one can say that it is the deliberate intention of modern political philosophy to try to modify the regime-character of politics altogether: to lessen the reliance on human character, and therefore the overt encouragement of specific character traits, and to rely instead chiefly on institutions, and on the minimal modifications of human behavior and outlook required by a civic virtue that is principally "self-interest rightly understood." Paradoxically, the aim constantly pursued, with enormous political and legal energy, by modern liberal politics at its deepest or most self-conscious is, the depoliticization of human existence. Or to put it in other terms, the modern liberal regime seeks to submerge its own regime character: the distinctive way of life and the restricted range of human types forcibly encouraged by liberal democracy is meant to appear to be the by-product of an openness to the greatest diversity of ways and types. But the distinctive human ways and characteristics actually fostered— tolerance, competitive and acquisitive entrepreneurial talent, the privatization of religious and moral demands, egalitarianism and individualism, etc.—have never been sufficient to provide the civic virtue needed in a republican form of government, even in a liberal republican form. And the various complex institutional arrange- ments suggested by a succession of great modern theorists (feder- alism, representation, separation of powers, the party system, etc.) have never gone as far as intended in obviating the need for both statesmanship of a high order and a public-spirited citizenry. So a major and persisting problematic of study rooted in Strauss has been the investigation and explanation of how, precisely, the mod- ern liberal project, depoliticizing as it is, has had to be modified, or has had to modify itself, in an attempt to incorporate essen- tial or abiding demands of humanity's political nature, made most visible in classical republican life and thought.[26]

The Judiciary

This overall approach to the study of American government is distinguished by the stress it lays on the observation that the higher judiciary, in the U.S. system, is uniquely delegated to de- liver a publicly reasoned justification of the fundamental consti- tutional law through which, above all else, the regime evolves. The most fruitful focus of study of the American judiciary is, ac- cordingly, not the "judicial behavior" fashionable in "scientific studies" (seeking to discover the subjurisprudential and therefore supposedly more predictable sources of judicial decisions) but rather judicial *reasoning* linked to judicial *statesmanship.* From a perspective informed by Aristotle, such statesmanship as well as study of such statesmanship comes to sight as needing, to a far greater degree than is usually recognized by contemporary law schools, an education in the law that sees law as derivative from the regime—and that sees the Constitution, not merely as "fun- damental law," but as the structuring of political powers that con- stitutes, and must be explained in terms of, the human purposes of our very specific regime. Helpful in opening the legal mind in this regard is a normative-comparative study of constitutionalism and constitutional jurisprudence in other contemporary liberal-democratic regimes besides the United States; and scholars influenced by Strauss in varying degrees have been at the forefront of this kind of study and teaching.[27]

The task of a genuinely empirical and rational-scientific study of the judiciary is that of examining, in the light of the standard set by the nature of our regime, the strengths and weaknesses of the arguments made by judges (and others involved with judging and judges), with a view to their civic implications and effects (discerned partly by looking to later political and legal consequences). This entails evaluative scrutiny, not only of the judicial opinions (and the dialogue among them), but also of the dialectically responsive words and deeds of the various legislatures and executives.[28]

Of the greatest importance are some of the earliest opinions and controversies, especially those involving the jurisprudence of John Marshall. These not only laid the groundwork of American constitutional jurisprudence. They were compelled to take far less for granted than is the case with contemporary jurisprudence. These original opinions wrestled with the expression in law of the unprecedented regime that had been newly founded. Led by Walter Berns, scholars who take their cue in some measure from Strauss argue for the superior wisdom of those early opinions, as opinions from which we still have much to learn—especially as regards the originating and fundamental purposes and nature of our regime as a whole, but also as regards the nature and practice of judicial review, the meaning of original intent, the proper legal and political status of religion, and the civic reasons that most fully justify (and thus correctly define the limits of) freedom of speech and religion as well as other basic rights.[29]

One may characterize what is distinctive about this kind of study of constitutional jurisprudence by saying that the focus is less on constitutional law than on the Constitution—interpreted not piecemeal, but as that legal core that more than anything else constitutes our specific regime (*politeia*) and its distinct way of life.

To understand the Constitution in this way is to look to its "original meaning" in an unusually profound and capacious sense: a sense that may have been understood only by a rare few of the most thoughtful among the Founders—and perhaps not fully even by them.[30] By the same token, it is not possible to plumb these depths of the philosophic thought underlying the Constitution without simultaneously calling into question key premises of that thought, in the light of the classical, and especially Aristotelian, alternative conception of republican life. The appeal to the wisdom of the framers is, in other words, not an invocation of authority but an invitation to critical dialogue at the highest possible level. Such dialogue with the Founders or their thoughts combines what Strauss called an "unhesitating loyalty to a decent constitution" (LAM, 24) with an intransigently clear-sighted recognition of the questionableness or possible inferiority (in the light of the classical republican alternative) of some of that constitution's most basic principles.[31] Such questioning is a cornerstone of Strauss's call for "moderation," including the moderating of our regime's more extreme inherent proclivities—to leveling egalitarianism, majoritarian tyranny, and individualism (a stress on rights at the expense of essential corresponding duties, including self-restraint).

An Aristotelian perspective spotlights, however, the deeply problematic fact that the function of the higher judiciary, and especially of the Supreme Court, is an essentially aristocratic function, uneasily situated within, and meant to temper, a basically democratic republic. This is not to go so far as to say that "judicial review is a *deviant* institution in the American democracy" (Bickel, 1962: 18; cf. Faulkner, 1978); but it is to suggest strongly that the practice of judicial review therefore requires, on the part of judges, a most delicate and circumspect judicial prudence. In this perspective, judicial deference to elected branches of government is far from being a mere concession to majority power; it is above all a manifestation of respect for the ultimate responsibility of the republican citizenry and its delegates. Scholars imbued with Aristotle's teaching have tended, on this civic republican basis, to look with concern and even alarm at the insufficiently thoughtful freedom with which judges have in recent decades arrogated to themselves unprecedented political power in modern democracy. This has led, among scholars influenced in some important degree by Strauss, to a very lively debate about the scope and legitimacy of judicial "activism"—that is, intervention by judges, through their decisions, in the political process, aimed at advancing what the judges conceive to be the ultimate ends proper to the American regime.

Berns (1976 and 1987), while recognizing the need to supplement the Founders' emphasis on individual rights with some greater measure of the classical concern for civic virtue and its sources in civil society (especially the family and religion), has stressed that a major feature of that classical virtue is the moderation that consists in remaining as faithful as possible to the guiding principles of a decent or respectable regime. In the American case, this entails fidelity and deference to the relatively moderate version of the regime of individual liberty and indirect majoritarian rule elaborated in the predominantly (though not exclusively) Lockean natural rights political theory and Montesquieuian constitutionalism of the Founders. Such fidelity requires, on the part of scholars, forceful argumentative restatement, and clarification, of that original political theory, in the face of our reigning historicist relativism and the consequent temptation to retreat to a shallow legal positivism. This entails, to be sure, exposure of limitations in, and hence even the questionableness, of our founding (predominantly Lockean) theory. It is absurd, however, to conclude (Berns insists) that this critical exposure of limitations grants judges a license to substitute, for the Founding vision and theory, their own comparatively half-baked visions, or the half-understood "up to date" theories of rights that they or their law clerks borrow, inevitably, from faddish and essentially relativistic or ultimately groundless contemporary academic theorizing.

In the last two generations, constitutional law in theory and in practice has moved fast and far from the position Berns has striven to defend.[32] The day has been largely carried by a judicial activism rooted in the slippery sands of relativistic and historicist academic moral theorizing. The question that has haunted American constitutional law for over a half century has been succinctly formulated by Thomas Grey (1975: 718): "does not the erosion and abandon-ment of the 18th century ethics and epistemology on which the natural-rights theory was founded require the abandonment of the mode of judicial review flowing from that theory? Is a 'fundamen-tal law' judicially enforced in a climate of historical and cultural relativism the legitimate offspring of a fundamental law which its exponents felt expressed rationally demonstrable, universal and immutable human rights?"

Sotirios Barber has responded by suggesting that this situation liberates us, in our conception of the goals of our constitution and regime, to go well beyond and above the Founders' conceptions —to interpret the Constitution as a vehicle for the fostering of a certain type of democratic civic virtue. Barber rejects Berns's ar-gument for judicial deference as untenable in our situation, and as likely to degenerate into legal positivism. Barber counters with what he calls an "aspirational" approach to constitutional jurispru-dence. By this he does not mean what the more sober Gary Jacob-sohn means when he argues, following Frederick Douglass and Lincoln and Martin Luther King, that we are true to the Founders' original intention when we credit them with intending to use con-stitutional language, in crucial sentences, that left room for future advances, beyond what they had yet achieved, and perhaps even conceived, but along the lines that they had laid down. Jacobsohn continues to insist that we can and should see in the Constitution what Hamilton insisted was there—the governmental instantia-tion of a specific regime of natural rights republicanism. But Jacob-sohn adds that we need not limit our civic aspirations to those of the Constitution, for, he submits, the Constitution does not claim to be the sole source of our aspirations, only the regulator of them: "what the Constitution aspires to will leave considerable space for the political application of additional aspirations—so long as they do not contradict constitutional design" (Jacobsohn, 1986: 139).

Barber, in contrast, contends that all citizens, even or espe-cially judges, but not only judges, can and must go far beyond the Founders' vision (whose limitations he does not, however, de-lineate or demonstrate).[33] "Virtue" is to be reinterpreted (in pro-foundly unclassical terms) as not simply the exercise of self-government, but such exercise as makes "honoring constitutional rights" (conceived as incapable of mutual conflict) the single "highest political value"—not to be abridged "no matter what the sacrifices" may be, as regards "national security, tranquility, and prosperity." Judges are to advance this moralistic agenda without any duty of deference to popular will as expressed through the elected representatives. But by the same token, judges cannot or ought not to expect to maintain their recently asserted "monopoly" on final determination of the constitutionality of law and governmental action: all branches, and even all citizens, can and ought to take (often rival) responsibility for such final determination.[34]

To this Brubaker has rejoined with the charge that, apart from the question whether this represents a legitimate enlargement, or in fact a dubious and immoderate transformation, of the regime's basic notions of virtue and of rights, Barber's individualist reading of citizenship is unrepublican and anarchistic. Barber (Brubaker submits) needs to take more seriously his own recognition that in a democratic republic, it is not the *individual* so much as the *people,* engaged in the contest of politics as a civic *community,* that properly exercises rational constitutional judgment, and does so through its elected representatives above all. What follows from this recognition, Brubaker contends, is the republican principle of judicial restraint or deference—given its classic formulation by Thayer: even when the court disagrees with the legislature's (and, in some cases, the chief executive's) interpretation of the Constitution, still, so long as the court finds the legislature's interpretation reasonable and defensible, rather than arbitrary or clearly mistaken, it ought to defer to that interpretation, since it is given by the people's chosen representatives. And more fundamentally, none of us, as individuals, can prudently demand or ought reasonably to expect from our community of fellow citizens the excessively theoretical and moralistic dedication to rights that Barber proposes.[35]

Brubaker does not take serious issue, however, with Barber's conclusion (leaving aside now how he reaches it) that none of the branches of government, including the judiciary, ought to monopolize final determination of constitutionality. This suggestion has been given its strongest formulation by Agresto (1984), who, relying heavily on the examples set by Lincoln and Franklin Roosevelt, insists on the legitimacy, in extreme cases, of legislative and executive defiance of Supreme Court decisions. To the trajectory of this line of argument, Leslie Goldstein (1991: 107, 109–10) has raised the following reservation: Lincoln, when he openly defied the Dred Scott decision, "limited" such defiance "to those constitutional positions" that (in Lincoln's words) had not been "fully settled," that had not been "affirmed and re-affirmed through a course of years." Agresto, Goldstein observes, "pointedly refrains from endorsing Lincoln's limit." She goes on to stress that, as Agresto himself brings out, the explicit constitutional powers over the judiciary that are given to the legislature are "unsuitable for altering particular decisions." This, together with a consideration of proposals regarding the relation of the Supreme Court and the other branches that were rejected by the Constitutional Convention, leads Goldstein to conclude that "the authors of the Constitution deliberately chose to keep from the hands of the lawmaking majority any direct, precise power to overrule the Court."

These debates may point to the thought that our constitutional frame, as designed by the Founders and directed by their ultimate moral purposes, calls for a mutual deference among the three branches, each respecting one another's distinctive sovereign strengths and hence proper share in final determination of constitutionality. To the maintenance of such a balance, a constitutionally responsible higher civil service may have an important contribution to make (as we shall see in a moment).

The Executive: The Presidency

A leitmotif of Strauss-inspired study of American politics has been critical evaluation of those presidents and would-be presidents in the course of whose careers the regime has undergone severe and to some extent transformative testing. Here are illuminated the evolving potentials and limits of the office, and its relation to the rest of the constitutional regime. Here are to be found explanations of the constraints upon, and measures by which to understand and to judge, the "man now in office"—while doing justice to both institutional and personal factors (Landy and Milkis, 2000; Lord, 1988). Yet presidential studies that take their bearings from Strauss have been distinguished by their warnings against focusing too narrowly on the office of the president (as in the classic work of Corwin, 1940), or on the officeholder and his acquisition and exercise of power (the sort of study made fashionable by Neustadt, 1980); those affected by Strauss have insisted on the need to study the presidency in the context of our entire constitutional regime, viewed in the large historical context of the struggle of modern thought since Machiavelli to find a republican substitute for monarchic or dictatorial energy of leadership. In Tulis's words (1987: 12), "to look at American politics from the perspective of the polity rather than the presidency allows one to see the dilemmas that attend the constitution of executive power in a republican regime."

The fundamental dilemma of the American presidency, Tulis contends, is caused by the populist redesign of the office that was effected by Woodrow Wilson, inspired in part by the successes of Theodore Roosevelt as a "rhetorical president"—but going deeply against the much less populist design of the Founders. The upshot has been, "Presidents inhabit an office structured by two systemic theories. Presidents are, as it were, caught between two layers of systemic thought"; "the two theories of the constitution do not fit together to form a coherent whole. Instead, elements of the old and new ways frustrate or subvert each other" (Tulis, 1987: 146). Against this, David Nichols (1994) has tried to show that all major elements of the presidency that emerged in the twentieth century are no more and no less than actualizations of ultimately harmonious potentialities implanted in the office by the framers or their founding.

This major controversy continues (see, e.g., Tatalovich, 2000). But as Nichols observes (1994: 1, 33–34, 169–70), both parties to this intra-Straussian debate share a fundamental critique of the reigning non-Straussian frameworks for study of the presidency. Those frameworks are defined by the assumption that the Founders established in the presidency an office whose powers are too weak to meet the challenges of modern "big" government. "Few people question the idea that the expansive powers of the 'modern Presidency' emerged in the twentieth century as an alternative to the cramped legal office created by the Constitution."[36] While "progressives" (led by Wilson and Croly)[37] drew from this the conclusion that the Founders must be overcome, the "restraintists" (led by Taft, 1916, and Corwin, 1940) reacted to the two Roosevelt presidencies by reaffirming what were argued to be the original constitutional restraints on executive power. As Nichols puts it, the "belief" shared by both opposing camps "that the constitutional Presidency is a weak Presidency" has "been questioned in the work of political scientists such as James Ceaser and the students of Herbert J. Storing. This third school claims that the framers of the Constitution intentionally established a strong constitutional Presidency." The dispute within this third school is over the extent to which the strength of the president was intended to rest on his popular rhetorical leadership (see esp. the critique by David Nichols, 1994: chap. 7 of Mansfield, 1989).

Underlying this is a still more fundamental dispute over the degree to which the framers feared and sought to curtail an excessive democratization of the constitutional regime. The issue is indeed one of degree; for few would deny that the framers were seriously intent on remedying the age-old defects of unchecked democratic —i.e., majoritarian, populist, and demagogic—politics. But scholars shaped by Strauss have distinguished themselves by proving that this deep concern of the framers was an expression, not so much of historical prejudice, as of far-seeing and powerful argumentation rooted in the history of republican thought and practice. Accordingly, a distinctive theme of such scholars' studies of presidential *selection* has been a quest to recover or discover institutional and civic resources that might help check the American regime's proclivity to drift toward more narrowly power-centered, populist, and demagogic conceptions of the presidency. Part of this effort has been the retrieval and elaboration of a Hamiltonian understanding of the presidency as a responsible republican substitute for monarchy. Looming large here are accounts, especially Mansfield's, of the evolution of the modern constitutional executive out of the struggle of the modern political philosophers to "tame" Machiavelli's conception of "the prince." In unpacking this dimension of the evolution of modern constitutional theory, light is shed not only on the nature of the presidency (as well as prime ministerial parliamentary leadership), but also on some of the conundrums of the modern political philosophers' attempts to overcome the limitations of the rule of law and of institutionalized rationality.[38]

The Executive: The Civil Service

Those who take their bearings from Strauss do not disregard the enormous role played by the more anonymous and undramatic lower echelons of the modern executive—"bureaucratic" politics or "public administration." But Strauss-oriented approaches to the study of public administration typically protest against, and try to repair, the scholarly tendency to pay insufficient heed to how much the natures of bureaucracies are decisively differentiated by the distinctive moral goals set by the particular regime—and by political struggles over defining the regime—in which bureaucratic politics operate.[39]

Still more importantly characteristic is the stress laid, in study of public administration that follows Herbert J. Storing's lead,[40] on resuscitating (against the prevailing tide of "scientific management") clear and capacious concepts of "the public interest"—as opposed to the public will or wants—and of "responsibility" to the public interest, especially in the education and in the conception of the calling of the civil servant. In 1964 Storing lamented:

The education of the civil servant is most deficient in its most important respect, and this includes not only his formal education but all of the instruction and advice aimed at him by the various representatives of the discipline of administration. The question of his responsibility—his duty, he may still say, especially if he is in military service—is that question about which the civil servant receives least instruction from his teachers and which is typically shrugged off with smug tolerance or superficial relativism. He is in fact taught irresponsibility in the most important cases. He is taught to look to two standards: technical competence and popular will; beyond these he has no business to venture—and there are no higher standards anyway. Yet it is where these standards are unavailable, or contradictory, or insufficient that he meets his most difficult and highest tests.[41]

In part through the influence, direct and mediated, of Storing and his students, most notably John Rohr (see esp. 1976, 1989, 1998),[42] there has been some improvement in this regard, at least in the available scholarly literature and academic teaching (see Rohr, 1990).

A corollary to this effort to counter "the conventions of American public life" and the "general opinions about what is respectable" that "tend to draw the civil servant back from his highest public duties rather than to guide him toward them" (Storing, 1964: 46) has been a search for ways to try to foster a distinctly American version of a "higher" or "senior" civil service that would have something in common with that of the United Kingdom and France: bureaucrats responsive to the commands of the elected government, who yet pose a moral counterweight because they are endowed with an ethos not of mere technical competence and "neutrality," but of self-conscious responsibility to and for the overarching national interest.[43] Taking the torch passed when Storing met his premature demise, Rohr has devoted his considerable energy to wrestling with the grave difficulty caused by the fact that, in his summary words (1995: xi), "Contemporary administrative institutions labor under a certain illegitimacy because their intellectual origins are traceable, not to the framers of the constitution, but to the anglophile civil service reformers of the late nineteenth century. These reformers—notably Woodrow Wilson and Frank Goodnow—considered the framers' principle of separation of powers a hopeless anachronism, which they rejected in favor of parliamentary principles. This, in turn, underlay their cardinal point on the distinction between politics and administration—a point that has both defined the academic field of public administration and thrown it into disarray." The "disarray" is most acutely seen in the deep unease over a role in the American polity for the civil service or public administration that, while remaining subordinate, is more than merely that of a tool.

Rohr has strenuously if controversially contended that the (qualified) independence and even the limited political activity of the civil service requires and implies no necessary rejection of the way the framers understood their principle of separation of powers. This is not to say that the administrative state as it has emerged over the years was envisioned by the framers, or that it simply carries out their vision. Rohr's contention is that the administrative state takes the place that was in some measure originally intended to be occupied by the Senate, as part of the framers envisaged "executive establishment." Relying heavily on an interpretation of the actual debates at the time of the Founding, and insights provided by Anti-Federalists as well as Federalists, Rohr argues that "with allowance in mind for the havoc two hundred years will wreak on anyone's intent" it can reasonably be said that "the function of the higher reaches of today's civil service is, in broad outline, a reasonable approximation to what the framers envisioned as the function of the Senate in the proposed regime"—given that "today's Senate resembles hardly at all the institution envisioned in the debate of 1787/88" (1986, 28, 39; see the context). He further argues that in its "representative" character—as a kind of microcosm of at least a substantial swath of the populace—today's civil service "heals a defect in the Constitution," a defect spotlighted by the Anti-Federalists (ibid., 46, 171).

On this basis, Rohr sketches the outlines of "a normative theory of Public Administration that is grounded in the Constitution." More precisely, he suggests that the civil service view itself much more self-consciously than is its wont as the protector of the constitutional system of the separation of powers, conceived in the flexible and prudent terms of the framers' vision: "Administrative agencies often do choose among constitutional masters, but they usually do so as a matter of fact and seldom as a matter of constitutional principle. Their preoccupation with the low arts of organizational survival blinds them to the better angels of their nature. They should lift their vision to see themselves as men and women who 'run a Constitution'" (ibid., "Conclusion," esp. 181–82).

The Legislative Branch, Political Parties,
and Public Policy Formation

Paradigmatic for the perspective on Congress distinctively growing out of Strauss is Bessette's (1994) insistence on the *deliberative* nature of legislative bodies. This approach opposes the fashionable analytic tendency to reduce congressional deliberations to "decisions" that express nothing more than the outcome of the perhaps quantifiable sum of the vectors of the tug and pull of interest-group struggle and the drive for reelection. Without denying the strength of these powerful forces, Bessette's type of analysis lays out the manifold evidence for a process in which reasoning in quest of compromises that serve the common good can supervene to mediate and to elevate the ever active, narrow, and self-serving interest-group struggle.[44] In this optic, the broad-based political parties are shown to be major contributors to the deliberative dimension of the interest-group struggle; and one can characterize political science influenced by Strauss as evincing unusually high respect for the two-party system in the United States, and even for rather unpopular practices (such as party-controlled redistricting) and otherwise questionable institutions (such as the electoral college) that arguably help to maintain or to strengthen the major parties.[45] McWilliams and others have highlighted the importance of parties in fostering an otherwise weak and threatened "fraternal," local or decentralized, and participatory dimension of democracy.[46] Jaffa's interpretation[47] of the evolution of party realignment has shown how the two-party system, strangely unforeseen at the Founding, is rooted in (though surely not wholly explained by) the irrepressible, if usually muted and, on the whole, healthy, continuation of regime differences, or of fundamental debate over the regime. This same analysis serves to underline the important function played in American civic development by dissenters from the existing regime.[48]

The Contribution Made by Dissenters

Indeed, radical "unofficial" opposition, and the moral challenges it forces upon the reigning regime, are seen in the Strauss perspective as shapers of regime evolution, and, even when the dissent fails, as uniquely revealing indicators of the nature of the regime.[49] It is no accident that the monumental work of Strauss-inspired study of American political thought is Storing's (1981) seven-volume *Complete Anti-Federalist,* assembling and commenting in depth upon the writings of those opposed to the ratification of the American Constitution in 1787;[50] or that the single most influential volume of Strauss-inspired "American politics" literature is Jaffa's account (1959) of the intellectual evolution of the two great radicals, Douglas and Lincoln—and their decisive debates, in which and through which the American regime began to be re-founded or transformed forever. McWilliams (1983; 1984; 1987), preeminently among those who have received some influence from Strauss, has richly clarified the contribution made by America's Puritan-based religious traditions, especially in their dissent from secular liberalism, to the moderation and amelioration of the tendency to social atomization that haunts modern democracy.[51]

This kind of study of the American regime has from the beginning spotlighted the challenge to the regime's moral self-definition posed by the core problem of race, and has made it a major project to recover African-American theorists, preeminently Frederick Douglass, but also theorists of "Black Nationalism" and "Black Power," in their dialogue with theorists of assimilation.[52] The way those influenced by Strauss view the writings of African-Americans is perhaps best articulated by Storing in the introduction to the volume of "Political Writings by Black Americans" that he edited (reprinted in Storing, 1995: 206–20). The "glass through which the black American sees" America "can distort." "Anger, frustration, hopelessness, confusion, excessive inwardness often result from the black's situation." But the glass

> can also provide a clean, sharp view of America, exposing its innermost and fundamental principles and tendencies, which are largely ignored or vaguely seen through half-closed eyes by the majority of white Americans, whose circumstances do not compel them to look at their country and to wonder about it. This does not mean that the black is necessarily revolutionary—most blacks are not; but it does mean that he takes seri-

ously the possibility of revolution, or rejection, or separation. He thus shares the perspective of the serious revolutionary. He appeals, at least in thought, from the imperfect world of convention and tradition (very imperfect, indeed, from his point of view) to the world of nature and truth. In important respects, then, black Americans are like a revolutionary or, more interestingly perhaps, a founding generation. That is, they are in the difficult but potentially glorious position of not being able to take for granted given political arrangements and values, of having seriously to canvass alternatives, to think through their implications, and to make a deliberate choice. To understand the American polity, one could hardly do better than to study, along with the work and thought of the founders, the best writings of the blacks who are at once its friends, enemies, citizens, and aliens. (ibid.: 207–8)

Not the least important contribution of African-Americans has been their meditation on "the ancient question of the relation between the political whole and its parts." Following the giants of early modernity, it has "been the view of many black American thinkers, as it has generally been the view of white American thinkers," that society is "an aggregate of homogeneous or undifferentiated individuals." There has, however, "also been a different line of argument, perhaps most fully and thoughtfully presented in Du Bois's early essay on 'The Conservation of the Races,' but explored also by Washington, Baldwin, and Carmichael": "that an individual is part of a series of increasingly larger groups, including family, community, race, and country." These "various social groups extend, define, and give significance to the individual; and they are in turn bound together in a diverse, mutually supporting and enriching whole." In this perspective, "social and political thought ought to aim to help men find their way into broader and higher levels of significance." The aim should be, however, "not to abandon the narrower, particular associations but rather, by sustaining their integrity and exploring their implications, to enrich and elevate the whole community." When "carried to its fullest extent, the argument suggests some basic questions, as Du Bois saw, about the accepted foundations of American government and politics and even about the accepted foundations of politics in the modern world" (ibid.: 218–19).

Interest Groups, Civil Society, and Cultural Criticism

The neoclassical approach to the study of interest-group politics and of "civil society" grows out of a new exegesis of Tocqueville's *Democracy in America*. This interpretation, opposing or subordinating more conventional "sociological" readings, insists on the philosophically inspired, and partially Aristotelian, character of what Tocqueville calls his "new science of politics."[53] The light cast by this science, so understood, does more than help illuminate how "associations" in modern democracy can function, in interaction with local government and political party participation, to sublimate private group interest into public interest (see, e.g., Storing and Self, 1963: 212–20). More specifically and controversially, what becomes prominent in the newly understood Tocquevillian societal analysis is the vacuum of meaning and of sources of dedication that looms as the greatest threat to the human spirit in American democracy. Seen from this kind of Tocquevillian perspective, the challenge of filling this vacuum calls for strengthening organized religion as well as organized parties, for preserving as much as can be preserved of traditional family mores and structure, and for the revival of democratic liberal education informed to some extent by an aristocratic goal—that is, aimed at excellence consisting in spiritual deepening and intellectual refinement as well as in character development and civic spirit.[54]

The most dramatic application of this perspective to cultural criticism of contemporary democracy is Bloom's explosive best seller (1987), whose impact proved the potential of this sort of political theory to reach out and to speak, with arresting power, to the spiritual perplexities of the broad mass of the reading public in our age. Presenting a dedicated teacher's "first-person" report on the soulless disintegration of the liberal arts in the university, Bloom offered, as an alternative, a vision of a liberating, erotic encounter with the Great Books, whose deepest unifying theme he explicated through a sustained meditation on the his-

tory of political philosophy since Socrates. (What was most original in Bloom's scholarship generally was his pioneering readings
of great works of literature as vehicles for affording vivid access,
in our parochially secular-democratic age, to the great alternatives
among regimes, among types of human excellence, and among
experiences of erotic passion and thought.)[55] Bloom argued that
the modern democratic hopes for participating in such a truly
liberal, because liberating, education are being washed away by
profoundly antidemocratic and antirational intellectual trends derived from protofascistic distortions of twentieth-century continental philosophy. The scholarly purveyors of these trends, which
have come to dominate the liberal arts in the universities, believe
themselves to be contributing to democracy while they inadver-
tently sap its essential moral and mental fiber. That Bloom had
struck a nerve became obvious from the thunderous howls of truly
febrile indignation that arose from the academic establishment.
The "culture war" (or wars) that Bloom's volcanic eruption ignited
do not cease to simmer and, periodically, to flare.[56]

Straussian-Tocquevillian concern to shore up or repair the pil-
lars of democratic health may be said to overlap with at least some
versions of "communitarian" critique and analysis. But the approaches that have been marked by Strauss's influence diverge
from the usual communitarian in at least three important (and not
necessarily harmonious) ways. In the first place, one finds among
those influenced by Strauss a greater inclination to respect, and to
seek to revitalize, the concern for individual autonomy, responsibility, and hence dignity retrievable from the older Lockean individualist and free enterprise philosophic tradition.[57] In the second
place, though admittedly at some real tension with the preceding, one is likely to find a greater reliance on family and religion,
and the familial and religious traditions in America, for counter-
weights to what are seen as excessively secular sources of individualism, materialism, and civic apathy or cynicism.[58] Thirdly, those
who take their orientation from Strauss fault many communitarians for their tendency to neglect how profoundly their continental philosophic sources are antiliberal, antiegalitarian, and anti-
democratic. Those in some measure educated by Strauss are far

from denying that something very important is to be learned from continental political theory's explicit and implicit critiques of liberal democracy in America; but they are apt to insist that the fully discomfiting character of those critiques needs to be confronted, so that we can learn from them what communitarians are prone to overlook—the dangers in the excesses of the democratic spirit itself, and not least in unchecked egalitarianism and egalitarian communalism.[59]

FROM CULTURAL CRITICISM TO THE FUNDAMENTAL QUESTIONS

Thus the critical theory of American civil society grounded in Strauss draws from and conduces to hermeneutic scholarship aimed at bringing to light the full force and depth of the late-modern critique, rooted in Rousseau, of Enlightenment rationalism in theory and in practice. First Rousseau, and then, successively, his more systematic if less intransigent German heirs, diagnosed the imperfections of the Enlightenment—with a view to refurbishing it and thus consummating its deepest (this-worldly) intentions. It was the apparent failure of these magnificent efforts that led Nietzsche to proclaim the need for a shattering transrational departure. But to what extent is this historical dialectic inevitable? And are its results necessarily as crisis prone as Strauss himself seems to have concluded? Can we not seriously consider a return to one or another stage of the unfolding drama, there to recover the essential complements that will make a reformed modernity, and perhaps a reformed America, unqualifiedly defensible? The challenge to modernity that Strauss laid down, in his opposition of ancients to moderns, continues to inspire manifold interpretative work—on Rousseau, Kant, Hegel, and Nietzsche. This scholarship follows with gratitude Strauss's lead, but often seeks, implicitly if not explicitly, to find a way to overcome his profoundly troubling critiques.

In other words, there is discernible in the work of many of those Strauss has shaped, a search, not always explicit (perhaps not even fully self-conscious), for a circumvention of the radical theses that express the core of his thought. This is most apparent in the fissures that have opened up among competing interpretations of the foundations of the American regime and of the Enlightenment rationalism that informs it.[60] Jaffa (and some of his followers) have gone so far as to argue that the American regime, centered on Lincoln, shakes off the contamination of modern philosophy (whose failure Strauss is conceded to have correctly diagnosed) through a quasi-divinatory recovery of Aristotelian praxis. Most others among the first generation of Strauss's students[61] have remained more soberly and modestly, if reluctantly, close to Strauss's own judgment. That judgment is indicated in his relentless essay on Locke (NRH) and in his brief but incisive remarks there and elsewhere on the distinctly modern principles animating the American regime (McWilliams, 1998).

Is it not possible, however, that the living presence of Strauss, and the reverence he naturally aroused, shielded his sober and modest students from facing, paradoxically, the very grave difficulties that his thought implies—and that he teaches must be faced? Strauss not only brought back to life the philosophic quest for final moral truth. Strauss deliberately resuscitated the possibility and the necessity of studying the American regime with genuine, and passionately hopeful, respect for its founding claim to be grounded on moral "truths" that are, or are deduced from what is, "self-evident": "the laws of Nature and of Nature's God." But Strauss also compelled the recognition that genuine respect for such a claim requires the most rigorous testing of its validity— leading perhaps to the discovery, in the process, of something of the utmost importance regarding one's own soul.

Now given Strauss's insistence on "the lowering of the goals" that comes to sight at the very heart of modern political thought; given Strauss's unmistakable inclination to judge modern rationalism to be ultimately a magnificent failure; given his "inclination" to judge classical philosophy to be, in contrast, decisively superior and more likely to be true; given also Strauss's more qualified endorsement of the superiority of ancient to modern practice (his meticulous account of Plato's *Laws* in its unvarnished analysis of life in the polis at its best—AAPL): given these intransigently severe features of Strauss's central contentions, I say, it is not surprising that those deeply affected by the serious initial hopes Strauss inspired should encounter sooner or later deeply troubled perplexity. It is understandable that even or especially those loyally indebted to and respectful of Strauss should find it hard, as dedicated citizens of America or of the West, to accept the critical detachment from the achievements of modernity, and from the love of one's own, that the logic of Strauss's critique demands. It is no wonder, then, that there has emerged a growing inclination among his followers to depart from Strauss: to challenge his relentless exposure of Locke's Hobbesian, un-Christian individualism; and to seek to discover in Locke, as well as in other early moderns, and thence in the theory and not only the practice of modernity, especially in America, a nobler, and even a more religious, outlook than Strauss's own analysis would seem to allow. By the same token, the question has been pressed, whether Strauss's unflattering judgment on modernity, in comparison with antiquity, can stand, once one faces squarely the harshness and inhumanity of the polis. Prominent here are the massive, though very different books of Rahe (1992) and Michael Zuckert (1994a), whose sophisticated historical erudition has greatly enriched, from somewhat divergent perspectives, our understanding of the precise stages in the evolution of republican thought leading to the American Founding.[62]

The great question is whether these restive quests, sensible enough on their own terms, for a way out of the Straussian problematic, do not spring from a failure to appreciate what was for Strauss the heart of the matter. That heart is the challenge posed by revelation, and the Socratic dialectical investigation of justice and nobility as the key to meeting that challenge, and thus as the grounding of the truly natural life for man: the contemplative life, consumed by the serene (if mortal and therefore melancholy) joy of the free investigation of the permanent nature of the beings and of their Author.

Efforts at achieving the appreciation of which I speak, through reenacting Strauss's confrontation with the Bible and with the capital texts of ancient and medieval rationalism, represent the most profound of the scholarly endeavors that carry forward

Strauss's approach to the study of politics. It is fair to wonder, however, whether any of us has yet fully plumbed the existential meaning of that "permanent human problem" to which Strauss sought to reawaken modern mankind. This problem, I believe Strauss was convinced by Socrates, has gnawed at the marrow, and has propelled the thinking, of every mind genuinely penetrated by the truth of the human condition. It is the lobotomizing of the modern brain's capacity to recognize this problem [63] — it is the "oblivion of eternity, or, in other words, estrangement from man's deepest desire and therewith from the primary issues" (WIPP, 55) — that Strauss saw as the soul-debilitating consequence that constitutes the decisive inferiority of modern thought and life to ancient (and medieval) thought and life at its peaks.

If Strauss is right, if this is indeed our historical situation, then each of us is confronted with a challenge that is daunting but that is not necessarily discouraging — for it is potentially invigorating. We must attempt to liberate ourselves from the peculiarly severe intellectual limitations of this age.[64] "We cannot be philosophers, but we can love philosophy"; such love in action "consists at any rate primarily and in a way chiefly in listening to the conversation between the great philosophers or, more generally and more cautiously, between the greatest minds, and therefore in studying the great books." But "here we are confronted with the overwhelming difficulty that this conversation does not take place without our help — that in fact we must bring about that conversation." Since "the greatest minds contradict one another regarding the most important matters, they compel us to judge of their monologues; we cannot take on trust what any one of them says." On the other hand, "we are not competent to be judges." "This state of things is concealed from us by a number of facile delusions." They add up to the delusion that "we somehow believe that our point of view is superior, higher than those of the greatest minds" — either because "our time, being later than the time of the greatest minds, can be presumed to be superior to their times"; or else because "we believe that each of the greatest minds was right from his point of view but not, as he claims, simply right": we assume that we know in some final way "that there cannot be *the* simply true substantive insight." We are thus induced to make fools of ourselves by "playing the part, not of attentive and docile listeners, but of impresarios or lion-tamers."

We have to try somehow to listen and also to judge, in full awareness of the drastic limitations of our very imperfect competence. "We have no comfort other than that inherent in this activity." "We cannot exert our understanding without from time to time understanding something of importance; and this act of understanding may be accompanied by the awareness of our understanding," by *noesis noeseos*—"so noble an experience that Aristotle could ascribe it to his God": "This experience is entirely independent of whether what we understand is pleasing or displeasing, fair or ugly. It leads us to realize that all evils are in a sense necessary if there is to be understanding. It enables us to accept all evils which befall us and which may well break our hearts in the spirit of good citizens of the city of God. By becoming aware of the dignity of the mind, we realize the true ground of the dignity of man and therewith the goodness of the world, whether we understand it as created or as uncreated, which is the home of man because it is the home of the human mind."

Notes

Abbreviations

For references to writings of Strauss, the abbreviations that follow
are used (full citations are given in the list of works cited).

AAPL	*The Argument and the Action of Plato's "Laws"*
CM	*The City and Man*
CPH	"On Collingwood's Philosophy of History"
GS	*Gesammelte Schriften*
HPP	*History of Political Philosophy*
HPW	*Hobbes' politische Wissenschaft*
LAM	*Liberalism Ancient and Modern*
NIPPP	"On a New Interpretation of Plato's Political Philosophy"
NRH	*Natural Right and History*
OT	*On Tyranny*
PAW	*Persecution and the Art of Writing*
PHPW	"Preface to *Hobbes' politische Wissenschaft*"
PL	*Philosophy and Law*
PPH	*The Political Philosophy of Hobbes: Its Basis and Its Genesis*
RCPR	*The Rebirth of Classical Political Rationalism*
SA	*Socrates and Aristophanes*
SCR	*Spinoza's Critique of Religion*
SPPP	*Studies in Platonic Political Philosophy*
TOM	*Thoughts on Machiavelli*
TWM	"Three Waves of Modernity"
WIPP	*What Is Political Philosophy?*

Introduction

1. Consider the fascinating autobiographical confession of the leading American pragmatist Richard Rorty, to the effect that his entire life's effort is a result of a failure to be able to follow Strauss's Platonism: "The Chicago faculty was dotted with awesomely learned refugees from Hitler, of whom Strauss was the most revered. . . . I read through Plato during my fifteenth summer, and convinced myself that Socrates was right—virtue *was* knowledge. . . . Socrates *had* to be right, for only then could one hold reality and justice in a single vision. Only if he were right could one hope to be both as good as the best Christians (such as Alyosha in *The Brothers Karamazov,* whom I could not—and still cannot—decide whether to envy or despise) and as learned and clever as Strauss and his students. So I decided to major in philosophy. . . . I wanted very much to be some kind of Platonist, and from fifteen to twenty I did my best. But it didn't pan out. . . . As I tried to figure out what had gone wrong, I gradually decided that the whole idea of holding reality and justice in a single vision had been a mistake—that a pursuit of such a vision had been precisely what led Plato astray. More specifically, I decided that only religion—only a nonargumentative faith in a surrogate parent who, unlike any real parent, embodied love, power, and justice in equal measure—could do the trick Plato wanted. . . . I decided to write a book about what intellectual life might be like if one could manage to give up the Platonic attempt to hold reality and justice in a single vision. That book—*Contingency, Irony and Solidarity*—argues that . . . one should abjure the temptation to tie in one's moral responsibilities to other people with one's relation to whatever idiosyncratic things or persons one loves with all one's heart and soul and mind (or, if you like, the things or persons one is obsessed with). . . . I do not think that I have more insight into the debates about or need for 'absolutes' now than I had when I was twenty, despite all the books I have read and all the arguments I have had in the intervening forty years. All those years of reading and arguing did was to let me spell out my disillusionment with Plato" (Rorty, 1993).

2. As was reported in the *Boston Globe* (May 11, 2003; and later in the *Economist,* July 19, 2003), an emanating source for the conspiracy

theories that sprouted in the American media was Lyndon La-Rouche, "fringe presidential candidate who believes that the world is being governed by Jewish bankers inspired by a Babylonian cult and that the Queen of England is a drug dealer": the "LaRouchites," the *Boston Globe* went on to observe, "argue that Strauss is the evil genius behind the Republican Party." The *Economist* remarked with bewilderment: "You might have thought that the [LaRouchite] article's overheated language and conspiracy-mongering would have killed the argument. But since then a flotilla of respectable publications, from *The New Yorker* to *Le Monde,* have jumped on the bandwagon." The *Wall Street Journal,* in a piece entitled "Joining LaRouche in the Fever Swamps" (June 9, 2003) quoted the boast of the LaRouche website: "Just weeks after the LaRouche in 2004 campaign began nationwide circulation of 400,000 copies of the Children of Satan dossier, exposing the role of University of Chicago fascist philosopher Leo Strauss as the godfather of the neoconservative war party in and around the Bush Administration, two major establishment publications have joined the exposé." LaRouche seems to have launched the "Satanic exposé" in a March 3, 2003, radio interview on the Jack Stockwell Show in Salt Lake City, which was followed by a long diatribe entitled "The Essential Fraud of Leo Strauss," published by LaRouche in his movement's organ on March 5, 2003. LaRouche's leading journalistic follower Jeffrey Steinberg was soon able to boast (*Executive Intelligence Review,* March 21, 2003), "Within days of the LaRouche interview, Leo Strauss was the subject of a series of public attacks, in the German, French and American media." In New York City there appeared (at The Public Theater) a play about the supposed Strauss conspiracy, entitled *Embedded,* by the Leftist actor Tim Robbins, which featured purported quotations from Strauss that turn out to be taken from the April 18, 2003, edition of LaRouche's *Executive Intelligence Review.*

3. See the concluding paragraph of Tim B. Müller, "Partei des Zeus: Die band—Der Einfluss der Straussianer auf die US-Politik," Feuilleton of the *Süddeutsche Zeitung,* March 5, 2003; the concluding paragraphs of Alain Frachon and Daniel Vernet, "Le stratège et le philosophe," *Le Monde,* April 15, 2003; and Pierre Hassner, "One

Year On: Power, Purpose and Strategy in American Foreign Policy: Definitions, Doctrines and Divergences," *National Interest* 69 (Fall 2002), 30–34, esp. n. 7 (Hassner's appeal to Strauss in his critique of the Bush foreign policy antedated by months the conspiracy theories attributing that policy to Strauss's influence). See also Hassner and Vaïsse (2003); Carole Widmaier, "Leo Strauss est-il néoconservateur? L'épreuve des textes," *Esprit* (November 2003), 23–38; Corine Pelluchon, "Leo Strauss et George Bush," *Le Banquet* (February 2004), 281–92; as well as Gerald Sfez, "Le véritable effet de Leo Strauss," *Le Monde,* December 8, 2002. It is worth noting that in an interview published in the *Daily Telegraph,* February 12, 2003, the Archbishop of Canterbury, Dr. Rowan Williams, had declared himself "very interested in conservative political theory of a classical kind," as exemplified by Leo Strauss, since the latter seemed "to have a real intellectual sense of what a conservative vision is which is not reactive, trivial or self interested."

4. The media in Germany and France exhibited greater sophistication; especially impressive, as a popular introductory glimpse of what Strauss and his legacy was all about, was the illustrated article in Germany's largest circulation newsmagazine *Focus*, Nr. 27 (June 30, 2003): 54–57: "Der Philosoph der Stunde" (the article was written by the distinguished editor of Strauss's *Gesammelte Schriften,* Heinrich Meier—who has also written illuminating introductions to each of the published volumes of the *Gesammelte Schriften* and important studies of Strauss: see Meier, 2005a and 2005b). See also, in Switzerland, Meier's "Rückhaltlos Fragen als Lebensform: Über die ursprüngliche Einsicht des Philosophen Leo Strauss," *Neue Zürcher Zeitung,* July 2/3, 2005; in France, Frachon and Vernet, 2004; and, in Italy, the articles about, and texts of speeches by, Meier and William Kristol to be delivered at the conference on Strauss at the Centro Studi Americani in Rome ("Leo Strauss: l'Uomo, il suo pensiero e la politica globale contemporanea"): *Il Foglio Quotidiano,* May 21, 2005.

5. As the *Economist* observed (June 19, 2003), "a little selective quotation can be used to give his thinking a decidedly sinister tinge. Strauss emphasised both the fragility of democracy and the importance of intellectual elites."

Chapter 1. Relativism

1. To take a prominent example from a leading spokesman for thoughtful contemporary opinion: Richard Rorty, while strongly siding with those who "persist in believing that a merely material and secular goal suffices: mortal life as it might be lived on the sun-lit uplands of global democracy and abundance" (1995, 89), nevertheless follows what he claims is the view of Whitman and Dewey, that "a classless and casteless society—the sort of society which American leftists have spent the twentieth century trying to construct—is neither more natural nor more rational than the cruel societies of feudal Europe or of eighteenth century Virginia" (1998, 30; see also 1998, 27–28, and 1991, 190 and 195, where Rorty admits that he has "not tried to argue the question of whether Dewey was right" in the fundamental value judgment for democracy—with which Rorty agrees and urges his reader to agree).

2. Some have reacted to our situation by falling back from reason to revealed religion as the ground and source of basic moral norms, and have even welcomed the bankruptcy of normative reason as the proof of the radical insufficiency of unassisted human reason and thus as the victory of religious orthodoxy, or of some sort of "political theology" over and against political philosophy. Having observed this development in his own religious dispensation, Strauss recognized early in his thinking career that "the victory of orthodoxy through the self-destruction of rational philosophy was not an unmitigated blessing, for it was a victory, not of Jewish orthodoxy, but of any orthodoxy, and Jewish orthodoxy based its claim to superiority over other religions from the beginning on its superior rationality (Deut. 4:6)" (LAM, 256). Something very similar could of course be said of Christianity, especially insofar as so much of orthodox Christian political theology appeals to natural law, the law of reason, as something distinct from and presupposed by revealed divine law. For the orthodox Christian as for the orthodox Jew, the divine gift of rationality must be rigorously used as the cornerstone of faith: faith completes and thus is partly founded on normative reason. It follows that it is "not sufficient for everyone to obey and to listen to the Divine message of the City of Righteousness, the Faithful City": in order to understand that message

"as clearly and as fully as is humanly possible, one must also consider to what extent man could discern the outlines of that City if
left to himself, to the proper exercise of his own powers"; "political philosophy is the indispensable handmaid of theology" (CM,
1). Yet it is surely not enough—and no thoughtful adherent of biblical orthodoxy ever supposed it to be enough—simply to assert or
to reassert the existence of natural law or right. Such law or right
must be rationally *proven* to exist. And in our time all the traditional
proofs appear to have lost their cogency, because they apparently
fail to meet the counterevidence and proofs to the contrary that
emerge from the new "experience of history"—our apparently new
experience of the severely conflicting diversity as well as mutability
of all cultural-historical norms. Our loss of confidence in normative reason includes or may even be said to be centered on a loss
of confidence in the capacity of unassisted reason to demonstrate,
on the basis of the available evidence about the human condition,
the universal and permanent validity of any fixed code of rational
laws or even moral principles.

The resulting situation is captured in a nutshell by Jacques
Maritain's report of the collective response by the UNESCO National Commission to a query about the agreement achieved on
"human rights" in preparation for the drafting and issuing of the
1948 Universal Declaration of Human Rights: "Yes, we agree about
the rights *but on condition that no one asks us why.*" As Maritain explains, the basic controversy was over the challenge to the idea of
natural or inherent rights presented by the "irreconcilable" view
that "man's rights are relative to the historical development of society, and are themselves constantly variable and in a state of flux"
(Maritain, 1950: 9 and 13). For a revealing account of the intense discussions that led to the deliberate dropping of all references to "nature" or "rights by nature" (which had been in the April 1948 draft)
from the final wording of the Preamble to, and the crucial Article 1
of, the 1948 Universal Declaration of Human Rights, see Morsink,
1999: 284–302, and Lindholm, 1992. René Cassin, the French vice-
chair of the four-person drafting committee for the Preamble, re-
calls that the phraseology that was adopted "allowed the Committee to take no position on the nature of man and of society and to
avoid metaphysical controversies, notably the conflicting doctrines

of spiritualists, rationalists, and materialists regarding the origin of the rights of man" (1972: 108). Lindholm's study of the drafting debate records (1992, 47, 50–51) leads him to find it "plausible to conclude that" the committee "wanted Article 1" to "neither assert nor to imply that the system of human rights is based on any conception of Human Nature"; the "essential piece of justification, drawn from the Preamble, is sociological and historical."

3. A few days before the fiftieth anniversary of the American Declaration of Independence, Jefferson wrote, in a famous letter (to Roger C. Weightman, June 24, 1826; in Jefferson, 1984: 1516–17): "May it be to the world, what I believe it will be (to some parts sooner, to others later, but finally to all), the signal of arousing men to burst the chains under which monkish ignorance and superstition had persuaded them to bind themselves, and to assume the blessings and security of self-government. That form which we have substituted, restores the free right to the unbounded exercise of reason and freedom of opinion. All eyes are opened, or opening, to the rights of man. The general spread of the light of science has already laid open to every view the palpable truth, that the mass of mankind has not been born with saddles on their backs, nor a favored few booted and spurred, ready to ride them legitimately, by the grace of God."

4. The phraseology Strauss uses is borrowed from Descartes, *Discourse on the Method,* and Bacon, *Great Instauration,* Pref.; *New Organon* 1.129, 2.31; *Advancement of Learning* 1.5.11; see also Benjamin Franklin's 1743 "Proposal for Promoting Useful Knowledge among the British Plantations in America," in Franklin, 1959–: 2.380–83.

5. For this and the next paragraphs, see CM, 3–5.

6. See OT, Introd., end (p. 27): "The manifest and deliberate collectivization or coordination of thought is being prepared in a hidden and frequently quite unconscious way by the spread of the teaching that all human thought is collective independently of any human effort directed to this end, because all human thought is historical."

7. Relativism as Strauss confronted it most immediately, in the 1950s and 1960s, especially in the Anglo-American world, was widely advocated and expressed in terms of a scientistic positivism that sought to construct a "value-free" social science that would express a neutral, nonevaluating objectivity—a kind of life raft on which philosophy and social science could save itself from the maelstrom

of the collapse of normative reason. Strauss engaged this scientistic positivism vigorously, but he always stressed that despite its temporary predominance, especially in the social sciences, it was bound essentially to collapse — and therefore would sooner or later in fact collapse — into the philosophically more serious, humanistic form of historicist or cultural relativism that denied the possibility of value-free objectivity. This prediction has been fulfilled. Positivism and its hope or dream of a value-free social science has gone out of fashion, even among its erstwhile prophets in academic political science. The leading theorists of our time are no longer positivists but rather historical and cultural relativists: not only the "postmodernists," and pragmatists (led by Richard Rorty: see esp. 1989: 115–16, 195–97; 1991: 190–95; 1998: 27–30), but also John Rawls (most explicitly in his later writings, esp. 1985, but already evidently in 1971: see 21, 46–50, 579–80, and above all 548, the culmination of the argument that provides the sole "Grounds for the Priority of Liberty" provided by the Rawlsian theory of justice — "We have to concede that as established beliefs change, it is possible that the principles of justice which it seems rational to choose may likewise change"; see also 4, 19, 35; but contrast 515–16). I will therefore focus on Strauss's engagement with this deeper, historicist relativism that has come to prevail in our time and largely ignore Strauss's refutations of the shallower scientistic positivism that was so pervasive in his immediate time.

8. John Dewey is a leading example of what Strauss has in mind (see Strauss's review of Dewey's *German Philosophy and Politics,* republished in WIPP, 279–81): the pervasive and decisive influence on Dewey of German philosophy of history and philosophy of science is well known. Writing in 1942, Dewey appealed against Nazism, and the deplorable "German heritage" Nazism embodied, to what Dewey still viewed as the superior German "experimental philosophy of life": "That such an experimental philosophy of life means a dangerous experiment goes without saying," but "the question of the past, of precedents, of origins, is quite subordinate to prevision, to guidance and control." It remains the case, Dewey avers, that "Germany is a monument to what can be done by means of conscious method and organization. An experimental philosophy of

life in order to succeed must not set less store upon methodic and organized intelligence, but more. We must learn from Germany what methodic and organized work means." 1942: 46–47, 140–42.

9. See, e.g., Dewey, 1939: 155–57: referring to "Jefferson's faith" in "the inherent and inalienable rights of man," Dewey declares that "the words in which he stated the moral basis of free institutions have gone out of vogue": we "forget all special associations with the word *Nature* and speak instead of ideals and aims." Yet Dewey adds that this must, somehow, be "backed by something deep and indestructible in the needs and demands of humankind." This absolutely crucial addition is never adequately explained or even investigated by Dewey (and is rudely and dismissively jettisoned altogether by Dewey's leading contemporary disciple today, Richard Rorty— 1989: 195–98): Strauss's entire project might be summed up, not too misleadingly, as the interrogation and clarification of what this addition means.

10. Consider Rorty, 1989: 195–97 ("we are under no obligations other than the 'we-intentions' of the communities with which we identify").

11. Cf. NRH, chap. 5, concluding para. (pp. 249–50) with John Locke, *Essay Concerning Human Understanding* 1.3.6 and 12, 2.20.2–3, 2.21.55 (and contexts); see also Thomas Jefferson, Letter to Thomas Law, June 13, 1814 (1984: 1338); "nature has constituted utility to man the standard and test of virtue" (see the context; but see also Letter to William Short, October 31, 1819 [1984: 1430–33]).

12. Berlin, 1958; Strauss's essay (originally published in 1961) is reprinted in RCPR, and the analysis of Berlin is in pp. 13–18.

13. Berlin, 1958: 8–9, 11, 15–16, 32, 38n, 46.

14. Strauss is paraphrasing ibid., 19.

15. Richard Rorty (1989: 46) emphatically reiterates and applauds Berlin's endorsement of this discriminatory definition of who are the civilized and who are the barbarians.

16. Cf. Strauss's comment in RCPR, 19: "A Marxist writer, Georg Lukács, has written a history of nineteenth- and twentieth-century German thought under the title *Die Zerstorung der Vernunft* [*The Destruction of Reason*]. I believe that many of us Western social scientists must plead guilty to this accusation."

17. The last two Latin words refer us, I believe, to reflection on the re-
lationship between the Aristotelians and the Platonists (see *Nicomachean Ethics* 1096a11–16).

18. A most helpful and penetrating supplement to Strauss's own writings on Plato and Socrates is Bruell, 1999; see also Bruell, 1994, as
well as Bolotin, 1979; Stauffer, 2001 and 2006.

19. Weber's most forceful statement of the conflict is found in the dramatic and famous close of his *Protestant Ethic and the Spirit of Capitalism*.

20. The quotations in what follows are from NRH, 145–46, and, above
all, PPH, 143–46 and 153 (= HPW, 138–40 and 148). This latter statement, in his book on Hobbes, is Strauss's first sustained adum-
bration of his decisive discovery concerning the nature of Socratic
philosophy—clarified by its opposition to Hobbes and to all modern thought growing out of Hobbes. The statement is, in Strauss's
words, "only a first attempt in this direction, and needs elaboration
in every respect" (PPH, 150 = HPW, 145); but it is one of the most
illuminating statements in this regard that Strauss ever penned
—while maintaining his meticulous sense of responsibility as a
writer. I would only add that in his statement in NRH, chap. 4, esp.
pp. 148ff., Strauss brings out more clearly the fact that our primary
opinions about justice in the full sense include the implication that
justice exists "only in a society in which everyone does what he can
do well and in which everyone has what he can use well"; that "justice is *identical* with membership in such a society and *devotion
to* such a society" (my italics); and that it follows that a "society is
just if its living principle is 'equality of opportunity,' i.e., if every
human being belonging to it has the opportunity, corresponding
to his capacities, of deserving well of the whole and receiving the
proper reward for his deserts," with the awareness that "the only
proper reward for service is honor" (here at p. 148 Strauss has a footnote that refers us to—among other texts—Cicero's *Republic* Bk. 3,
sec. 11, a passage that he has previously cited at p. 134n: "justice is
that virtue which, beyond others, is entirely devoted and applied to
the utility of others"; a bit later, in 152n, Strauss asks us to recon-
sider this passage for a third time, now in conjunction with *Republic* Bk. 6, sec. 29).

21. *"aber Einstimmigkeit und Verständigung eines jeden mit sich selbst*

und mit den anderen allererst ermöglichenden und so sich als wahr erweisenden Sinne festgehalten werden." Strauss's earlier reference is to be consulted at this point also: "cf. *Republic,* 457b and *Crito,* 46d–e."

22. *"diese wirkliche Einigkeit der letze Grund jeder möglichen Einigkeit ist."*

23. "This is admitted at least by virtuous *youths,* when they seek teachers of virtue, seek to *become* virtuous, and thus express that they have not virtue. What the youths confess of themselves is true of *all* men, if one is only *exact* [*genau*] enough, if one only considers accurately/exactly [*nur genau genug*] what speech means by virtue —virtue as completely unalloyed with vice. The virtue which is not found in the *works* of men is found in *speech* alone, in the divinatory, 'supposing' and 'founding' knowledge incorporated in speech."

24. Strauss refers us to: "*Symposium,* 212a; *Theaetetus,* 176c; *Republic,* 536a."

Chapter 2. The Revival of Classical Political Philosophy

1. Quotations in this and in the following two paragraphs are from NIPPP, 327–31.

2. For striking illustrations of how the unselfconscious modern philosophic preconceptions of famous classical scholars have led them to badly mistranslate Plato's *Republic,* see Bloom, 1965: Preface.

3. The generally flimsy character of the attempted critical responses to Strauss is nowhere more vividly on display than in a polemic written for the *New York Review of Books* (May 30, 1985) by an English classicist named M. F. Burnyeat. Proclaiming that he is going to "show that Strauss's interpretation of Plato is wrong from beginning to end," Burnyeat manages to articulate, amidst a flurry of polemical assertions, an attempted refutation of only one sentence in Strauss. The sentence in Strauss is: "the philosophers cannot be persuaded, they can only be compelled to rule the cities" (CM, 124). Burnyeat notes that Strauss adduces five specific passages in Plato's *Republic* as supporting evidence: 499bc, 500d4–5, 520a–d, 521b7, 539e2–3. But Burnyeat bases his purported refutation of Strauss's contention on an analysis of only one of these, 520a–d. In doing so Burnyeat commits a gross logical blunder (as was pointed

out in letters to the editor published in subsequent issues of the *New York Review of Books*). For in the sentence of Strauss quoted, the mention of "the cities" makes it clear that here Strauss is speaking of the difficulty that the regime ruled by philosophers could only come into being through the transformation of one or another of the actually existing cities. Strauss is pointing out that the philosophers, who would have to persuade or compel the nonphilosophers to let them take over an actual city, are themselves described by Plato's Socrates as having to be compelled by someone else to rule. Burnyeat claims, however, that the text of 520a–d shows that "it is the requirements of impartial justice that persuade them to govern *in the first place*"; "these devotees of pure reason are compelled to rule by the force of the reasoned argument." What "reasoned argument" is Burnyeat talking about? "The argument is" (Burnyeat claims) "that the philosophers owe a debt to the ideal city for providing the liberal education" that "teaches them to know and love justice." This is our classicist's extremely loose paraphrase of the words Plato wrote stating the argument Socrates says (at 520a–d) he would use to reconcile philosophers to take their turn at ruling *in a city already ruled by philosophers,* i.e., assuming that the city already has come into being and has existed for at least a generation, and that the philosophers being addressed owe their nurture to the city! What is more, in this very passage, Socrates goes on to emphatically declare that in any *other* city, a philosopher would rightly, according to impartial justice, refuse to rule. These are the actual words of Socrates in the passage (520a9–b4): "when the philosophers come to be in the other cities they quite reasonably do not participate in the labors in those cities. For they grow up spontaneously against the will of the regime in each city; and a nature that doesn't owe its rearing to anyone has justice on its side when it is not eager to pay off the price of its rearing to anyone."

4. See above all the speeches of Socrates, in Plato's *Phaedrus,* and of Diotima, as reported by Socrates, in Plato's *Symposium,* as well as the discussion of divinity in which Aristotle's *Nicomachean Ethics* culminates (Book 10).

5. See "On Classical Political Philosophy," in WIPP, 87–88: " 'The best political order' is, then, not intrinsically Greek: it is no more intrinsically Greek than health, as is shown by the parallelism of

political science and medicine. . . . When Aristotle asserted that the Greeks had a greater natural fitness for political excellence than the nations of the north and those of Asia, he did not assert, of course, that political excellence was identical with the quality of being Greek or derivative from it; otherwise he could not have praised the institutions of Carthage as highly as the institutions of the most renowned Greek cities. . . . Xenophon went so far as to describe the Persian Cyrus as the perfect ruler, and to imply that the education Cyrus received in Persia was superior even to Spartan education; and he did not consider it impossible that a man of the rank of Socrates would emerge among the Armenians." See also CM, 30.

6. Strauss appends the following footnote reference to the texts: "*Eth. Nic.* 1094a18–28, 1095a14–20, 1098a15–17; *Politics* 1252a1–7, 1278b21–24, 1324a5–8, 1325b14–32." In the pages that follow (CM, 32–35), Strauss raises and answers the question, how the modern "liberal" society's self-understanding is to be judged when viewed from the classical "liberal" perspective.

7. LAM, 4–5, 10–13, 15, 21; NRH, 140–43; cf. the sixth book of Aristotle's *Politics*.

8. CM, 35; we may add that the most obvious feature of contemporary democracy that bears out Strauss's characterization of it as being, in empirical fact, quasi-aristocratic, is the modern liberal judiciary.

9. CM, 19–20: "while the roots of the whole are hidden, the whole manifestly consists of heterogeneous parts. One may say that according to Socrates the things which are 'first in themselves' are somehow 'first for us'; the things which are 'first in themselves' are in a manner, but necessarily, revealed in men's opinions. . . . The highest opinions, the authoritative opinions, are the pronouncements of the law. The law makes manifest the just and noble things and it speaks authoritatively about the highest beings, the gods who dwell in heaven. The law is the law of the city; the city looks up to, holds in reverence, 'holds' the gods of the city. The gods do not approve of man's trying to seek out what they do not wish to reveal, the things in heaven and beneath the earth. A pious man will therefore not investigate the divine things but only the human things, the things left to man's investigation. It is the greatest proof of Socrates' piety that he limited himself to the study of the human

things. . . . Yet the opinions however authoritative contradict one another. . . . It becomes then necessary to transcend the authoritative opinions as such in the direction of what is no longer opinion but knowledge. Even Socrates is compelled to go the way from law to nature, to ascend from law to nature. But he must go that way with a new awakeness, caution, and emphasis. He must show the necessity of the ascent by a lucid, comprehensive, and sound argument which starts from the 'common sense' embodied in the accepted opinions and transcends them; his 'method' is 'dialectics.'"

10. "On Classical Political Philosophy," in WIPP, 92–94: "The philosophers, as well as other men who have become aware of the possibility of philosophy, are sooner or later driven to wonder 'Why philosophy?' Why does human life need philosophy, why is it good, why is it right, that opinions about the whole should be replaced by genuine knowledge of the nature of the whole? Since human life is living together or, more exactly, is political life, the question 'Why philosophy?' means 'Why does political life need philosophy?' This question calls philosophy before the tribunal of the political community: it makes philosophy politically responsible. . . . To justify political philosophy before the tribunal of the political community means to justify philosophy in terms of the political community, that is to say, by means of a kind of argument which appeals not to philosophers as such, but to citizens as such. To prove to citizens that philosophy is permissible, desirable or even necessary, the philosopher has to follow the example of Odysseus and start from premises that are generally agreed upon, or from generally accepted opinions (Xenophon, *Memorabilia* IV 6, 15): he has to argue *ad hominem* or 'dialectically.'"

11. CM, 20–21: "In its original form political philosophy broadly understood is the core of philosophy or rather 'the first philosophy.' It also remains true that human wisdom is knowledge of ignorance: there is no knowledge of the whole but only knowledge of parts, hence only partial knowledge of parts, hence no unqualified transcending, even by the wisest man as such, of the sphere of opinion. This Socratic or Platonic conclusion differs radically from a typically modern conclusion according to which the unavailability of knowledge of the whole demands that the question regarding the whole be abandoned and replaced by questions of another kind,

for instance by the questions characteristic of modern natural and social science. The elusiveness of the whole necessarily affects the knowledge of every part. Because of the elusiveness of the whole, the beginning or the questions retain a greater evidence than the end or the answers; return to the beginning remains a constant necessity. The fact that each part of the whole, and hence in particular the political sphere, is in a sense open to the whole, obstructs the establishment of political philosophy or political science as an independent discipline."

12. "In asserting that man transcends the city, Aristotle agrees with the liberalism of the modern age. Yet he differs from that liberalism by limiting this transcendence only to the highest in man. Man transcends the city only by pursuing true happiness, not by pursuing happiness however understood" (CM, 49).

13. PAW, 34; Strauss refers us to Cicero's *Tusculan Disputations* 2.4 and Plato's *Phaedo* 64b and *Republic* 520b2–3 and 494a4–10.

14. In what has come down to us as Plato's "Seventh Letter" we read (341): "If it appeared to me that it could be written and articulated adequately for the many, what finer achievement would there have been in our life than to write a work of great benefit to mankind and to bring nature to light for all? I do not, however, think the attempt to tell mankind of these matters a good thing, except in the case of some few who are capable of discovering the truth for themselves with slight indication." And in the "Second Letter" (314): "It is impossible for what is written not to be broadcast. That is the reason why I have never written anything about these things, and why there is not and will not be any written work of Plato, and why those now so called are of Socrates, having become beautiful and young. Be strong and trust me, and first read this letter many times and then burn it." Strauss refers us also to *Timaeus* 28 c3–5.

15. "This is not to deny that some great writers might have stated certain important truths quite openly by using as mouthpiece some disreputable character: they would thus show how much they disapproved of pronouncing the truths in question. There would then be good reason for our finding in the greatest literature of the past so many interesting devils, madmen, beggars, sophists, drunkards, epicureans, and buffoons." PAW, 36; see also the beginning of al-Fārābī's *Summary of Plato's "Laws."*

16. Beautiful and prominent examples are Plato's *Crito,* and Aristotle's account in his *Nicomachean Ethics* (1129b11–26) of the relation between law and the virtue of justice in the fullest sense.

17. WIPP, 227 (quoting Sabine, 1953); the historicist theoretician R. G. Collingwood, whose lucid articulations Strauss appreciated, suggested calling these "presumptions" the "absolute presuppositions" that lock each thinker in his age by determining the questions that he can ask: see Collingwood's "logic of question and answer," as sketched in Collingwood, 1970, chap. 7, esp. pp. 66–67, and Strauss's review essay (CPH) on Collingwood's *Idea of History.*

18. In reply to a critic who had seriously misunderstood the thesis on esoteric writing by supposing that it implied that all careful thinkers or philosophers engage in esoteric writing, Strauss stressed that he had not attributed esoteric writing to all "careful philosophers" (e.g., not to Kant) but only to some among the "careful philosophers" who were also "careful *writers,*" especially those whose works are "carefully written in the sense in which the *Discorsi sopra la prima deca di T. Livio* are carefully written, to say nothing of certain pre-modern books": WIPP, 230.

19. PAW, 159–61. For some important applications of Strauss's approach to the study of the relation of philosophers to their historical contexts, together with critiques of major contemporary upholders of the conventional scholarly approach to this question, see Ahrensdorf, 1994; Newell, 1987; Rahe, 2000; Sullivan, 1996 and 2004; Tarcov, 1982a and b and 1983b; Zuckert, M., 2002, chaps. 1–3.

Chapter 3. The Rediscovery and Reassessment of the Foundations of Modernity

1. Thus Richard Rorty insists that the famous rallying cries that express the principles of Enlightenment humanism must now be seen as no more than "handy bits of rhetoric": "the right way to take the slogan 'We have obligations to human beings simply as such' is as a means of reminding ourselves to keep trying to expand our sense of 'us' as far as we can." But how far is that? And what kind of "expansion" are we speaking of? "Expansion" here means something closer to absorption or even domination than to genuine openness, or mutually instructive dialogue with those who do not accept our liberal premises: "if one reads that slogan in the right

way, one will give 'we' as concrete and historically specific a sense as possible: It will mean something like 'we twentieth-century liberals.'" We must recognize that strictly speaking, "we are under no obligations other than the 'we-intentions' of the communities with which we identify." Rorty is certain that we can no longer take seriously the idea that there is a universal truth that can be reached by philosophic reasoning and argument: "if one reads" the "slogan" in "the wrong way, one will think of our 'common humanity' or 'natural human rights' as a 'philosophical foundation' for democratic politics. . . . —as if philosophers had, or at least should do their best to attain, knowledge of something less dubious than the value of the democratic freedoms and relative social equality which some rich and lucky societies have, quite recently, come to enjoy" (1989, 195–97).

2. A model of engaged civic learning that draws a major inspiration from Strauss or his outlook is Marc Plattner's role as cofounder, editor of, and contributor to, the *Journal of Democracy,* the organ of the National Endowment for Democracy.

Chapter 4. Strauss's Legacy in Political Science

1. Strauss, TOM, 13, 120–22, 207–8, 218, 252–53, 289–90; NRH, 177, 206–7; CM, 11.

2. The obvious models here are Plato's *Laws,* Aristotle's *Ethics, Politics,* and *Rhetoric,* and Cicero's *Republic* and *Laws* as well as his ethical and rhetorical treatises. The works of Xenophon are of a specifically delightful literary subtlety that puts them in a class by themselves. See also Bartlett, 1996; Ceaser, 1990; Danford, 1978; Ruderman, 1997a; Salkever, 1991; Hennis, 1963; Mahoney, 1992.

3. Strauss, WIPP, chap. 3; RCPR, chap. 1; and Storing, 1962: esp. 308–11, as well as 124–32 and 317–18; for a paradigmatic application to the American polity, see Brubaker, 1998.

4. Strauss invokes the words with which Tocqueville concludes his Introduction to *Democracy in America:* "I undertook to see, not differently, but further than the parties" (Strauss, WIPP, 81n). See also Miller, 1999.

5. For major Strauss-influenced critiques of some leading instances of the distortion of political science as well as civic and legal prudence by dubious contemporary theorizing, see Bartlett, 1996 (on

contemporary political development studies); Berns, 1962 (on voting studies); Bloom, 1975 (on Rawls); Brotz, 1974 and 1979 (on sociological methodology); Ceaser and McGuinn, 1998 (on multicultural education theory); Eden, 1987 (on historicism); Hamburger, 1990 (on utilitarianism); Miller, 1971 (on systems theory) and 1972 (on positivistic political science); Nichols, 1990 (on Pragmatism); Orwin and Stoner, 1990 (on Rawls, Dworkin, and Nozick); Pangle and Ahrensdorf, 1999 (on the neo-Realism of Waltz); Weinstein, 1962 (on the Group approach to political science); Zuckert, M., 1981 and 1994b (on Rawls, Nozick, and Ackerman).

6. For critical assessments, from Strauss-informed perspectives, of the strengths and limitations of "rational choice" or "positive political theory" and "the economist's view of the world," see Ceaser, 1990: 78–87; Dobbs, 1987; Forbes, 2004; Mansfield, 1990; Rhoads, 1985; Wilson, J., 1990; Zuckert, C., 1995; and the debates between Riker and Tulis (in Tulis, 1991a and Riker, 1991a and 1991b) and between Dobbs and Grafstein, 1988. The ongoing, never-ending, profound uncertainty and rather shallow debate that haunts contemporary political science's self-consciousness about its unsatisfactory foundations and methods is on display in Sartori, Laitin, and Colomer, 2004.

7. The most obvious example nowadays is the absurd incapacity of "rational choice theory" to account for the fact that people vote in large numbers in elections in contemporary democracy (what is known in the rational choice literature as the "paradox of voting turnout"); rational choice theory cannot escape concluding on its own premises that the costs and benefits of voting make it seem unlikely that more than a few citizens should turn out to vote — when, of course, they in fact turn out by the millions on a regular basis. For recent discussions, see Blais, 2000, and Verba, Schlozman, and Brady, 2000.

8. Strauss, WIPP, 33–36; CM, 30–35, 45–49; NRH, 135–45.

9. Strauss, WIPP, 34–35; CM, chap. 2; Bartlett, 1994 and 2001: chap. 6; Bruell, 1994; Strauss and Kojève, 1991: 187–88.

10. A major enterprise of followers of Strauss has been the execution of the first meticulously accurate translations into English of many or most of the great classics of political theory—which hitherto had been available only in very loose renderings, filled with inaccura-

cies in detail; recently the massive work of completing such a truly satisfactory translation of Tocqueville's masterpiece has been completed by Mansfield and Winthrop, 2000, who have appended to their translation a most helpful introductory essay: a similarly precise translation of well-selected crucial excerpts was executed by Grant, in Kessler, 2000.

11. Strauss, LAM, 4–5, 10–25; RCPR, 6; for other revealing critical comments of Strauss on liberal democracy, see esp. ibid., 15, 23–25, 263–64, 271–72, and WIPP, 36–38, 306–11. A very helpful brief characterization and assessment of Strauss's relation to American democracy is McWilliams, 1998.

12. NRH, chap. 2 (for helpful analysis, see Behnegar, 1997; for a qualified defense of Weber in response to Strauss, see Aron, 1957).

13. See esp. Ceaser, 1990; Mansfield, 1978, 1990, and 1991: chaps. 1 and 11.

14. For illuminating specific applications, see Rhoads, 1980 and 1993; Tatalovich, 1995.

15. Alvey, 1999 and 2001; Canavan, 1995; Cropsey, 1957 and 1977; Danford, 1980 and 1990: chaps 7 and 9; Griswold, 1998; Lerner, 1987: chap. 6; Mansfield, 1979 and 1991: chap. 11; Minowitz, 1993a and 1993b; McNamara, 1998; Nichols and Wright, 1990: chaps. 1–3, 5, 10; Plattner, 1982 and 1990; Rahe, 1992: Part 3; Shulsky, 1991a; Stavely, 1972; Stavely and Vinnicombe, 2002.

16. Bessette and Tulis, 1981: chaps. 8–9; Forde, 1989; Frisch and Stevens, 1971; Jaffa, 1959 and 1975; Krause, 2002; Mahoney, 1996; McNamara, 1999; Ruderman, 1997a and 1997b.

17. Walzer, 1977: chap. 1; for similar views of Thucydides expressed by influential contemporary theorists, see Morgenthau, 1958: 67; 1978, 8–9, 38–39; Waltz, 1959: 159–60, 210–12, 216; 1979: 66, 127, 186.

18. Strauss, CM, chap. 3; Bolotin, 1987; Bruell, 1974; Lee, 2002; Orwin, 1994; Palmer, 1992.

19. Ahrensdorf, 1997; Busch, 2004; Forde, 1992b and 1995; Frost, 1996 and 1997; Goldwin and Licht, 1990; Hassner, 1995 and 2003; Horelick and Rush, 1966; Johnson, 1993; Pangle and Ahrensdorf, 1999: chaps. 7–8; Rabkin, 1997; Shulsky, 1991b.

20. Berns, 1984: chaps. 3 and 5; Faulkner, 1990; Forde, 1998; Hassner, 1961 and 1997; Knippenberg, 1989; Orwin, 1996 and 2000; Pangle

and Ahrensdorf, 1999: chap. 6; Plattner, 1984; Rabkin, 1997, 1998a, 1998b, and 2005; Tarcov, 1988, 1989a, 1989b, and 1990.

21. Fukuyama, 1989 and 1992; for the most thoughtful replies to Fukuyama, see Burns, 1994, as well as the responses collected in the *National Interest* 16 (1989); for a helpful introduction to Kojève's neo-Hegelian political thought, see Frost, 1999.

22. Elazar, 1998a; Frost, 1997; Goldstein, 2001; Hassner, 1995 and 1997; Plattner, 2002.

23. The most important contributions to the Strauss-guided elucidation of the Founding ideas include Berns, 1976 and 1987; Bloom, 1990a; Diamond, 1992 (on whose thought see Zuckert, M., 1999); Epstein, 1984; Flaumenhaft, 1992; Forde, 1992a; Frisch, 1978; Frisch and Stevens, 1971; Goldwin, 1990 and 1997; Horwitz, 1986; Jaffa, 1965: chap. 2; Lerner, 1979 and 1987; Kurland and Lerner, 1986; Lindsay, 1991; Malbin, 1981; McDowell, 1998; McDowell and Noble, 1997; McNamara, 1999; Paynter, 1996; Rahe, 2005: Part Three and Part Two, chap. 6; Rosen, 1999; Rossum and McDowell, 1981; Stevens, 1997: Part Two; Storing, 1981 and 1995: Part One; Thompson, C. Bradley, 1998a and 1998b; Wilson and Schramm, 1994; Wirls and Wirls, 2004; Zuckert, M., 1996; Zvesper, 1977 and 1984. What sets apart Strauss-inspired study of the Founding and subsequent great American debates is captured well in Storing's Introduction to his study of the Anti-Federalists (1981: vol. 1, p. 4): his will be "an attempt to examine the thought, the principles, the argument of the Anti-Federalists, as they were understood by the Anti-Federalists themselves and by the other men of that time. . . . The aim will not be a history of the Anti-Federal movement or an analysis of its economic, sociological, or psychological underpinnings. We shall try to avoid presupposing some external set of questions or framework of analysis. Rather, we shall try to proceed from inside Anti-Federal thought, seeing the questions as they saw them, following the arguments as they made them. We shall explore the different levels of Anti-Federal theorizing, working our way critically through and if necessary beyond them, but always with the idea that the Anti-Federalists may have something to teach."

24. The work of Stoner (1994, 1998, and 2003) has brought into relief the evolving significance of the English common law for the American Founding and Constitution; pathbreaking in this regard was

Storing's incisive analysis (1995) of the quiet Montesquieuian revolution in English law effected by Blackstone.

25. See esp. Jaffa, 1959 and 1965: chap. 2; also Jacobsohn, 1986: esp. 95–112; Tulis, 1991b; Zuckert, M., 1998.

26. See esp. Banfield, 1970, 1974, and 1992; Berns, 2001; Diamond, 1992: chap. 21; Krause, 2002; Lord, 2003; Mahoney, 1996; Manent, 1998: Part Six; Mansfield, 1964, 1965a, 1965b, 1968, 1978: chap. 1, 1981, 1991: Part Three, 1996: chaps. 3, 6, 10; McNamara, 1999.

27. Elazar, 1990; Glendon, 1987 and 1989; Goldwin and Kaufman, 1988 and 1989; Goldstein, 2001; Hinchman and Hinchman, 1998; Jacobsohn, 1983 and 2003; Rohr, 1995 and 1998: Part Five.

28. Goldstein, 1992; Landy and Levin, 1995; Lerner, 1987; McDowell, 1982; Melnick, 1983 and 1994; Rabkin, 1989.

29. Berns, 1957, 1976, 1984: chaps. 2 and 15, and 1987; Brubaker, 1985a and Brubaker and Barber, 1987; Canavan, 1971; Clor, 1969 and 1971; Faulkner, 1968; Frisch and Stevens, 1971; Goldstein, 1991; Jacobsohn, 1977; Malbin, 1981; McDowell, 1981; Orwin and Stoner, 1990.

30. See Glenn, 1999: 198 (characterizing Berns's understanding in contrast to that of "originalists like Bork or Rehnquist"): "What 'the majority' of the founders understood particular clauses to aim at is less these clauses' constitutional meaning" than is "what the most philosophically insightful founders (primarily Jefferson and Madison) understood the Constitution as a whole to aim at." The "Constitution is more fundamentally what its general tendency is," than "what its authors meant by specific provisions." See also Wolfe, 1986 and 1996. Michael Zuckert, challenging the reigning consensus, has presented a detailed historical study showing that behind the Reconstruction or Post–Civil War Amendments (especially the 14th) there does lie a discernible, coherent intentionality that should have and perhaps still could guide jurisprudence (1986, 1987, 1993, and 1998).

31. See esp. Berns, 1957, 1976: 60–79, and 1987: 11–12, 157, 162, 167, 170, 173, 180, 241 (see also Glenn, 1999: 200–201 — on Berns); Goldwin, 1980b and Goldwin and Schambra, 1982.

32. For a helpful narration of major stages and problems in the development, see Goldstein, 1991: chaps. 4–5.

33. Except in very sketchy and polemical remarks in his critique of Berns (Barber, 1986).

34. Barber, 1986 and 1984: esp. 40, 55–57, 105–106, 117ff., 140–41, 165, 218–19; Brubaker and Barber, 1987.

35. Brubaker, 1985a, 1985b, 1985c, and 1998; Brubaker and Barber, 1987.

36. For a leading statement of the conventional view, see Greenstein, 1978, and also Greenstein, Berman, and Felzenberg, 1977.

37. See Wilson, W., 1908 and Croly, 1915, as well as Ceaser, 1979 and Wolfe, 1979.

38. Bessette and Tulis, 1981; Ceaser, 1979; the papers by Koritansky, Scigliano, Schmitt, and Slonim in Cronin, 1989; Crovitz and Rabkin, 1989; Diamond, 1992: chaps. 4 and 15; Flaumenhaft, 1992; Frisch and Stevens, 1971; Kautz, 2003; Lord, 2003; Mahoney, 1996; Mansfield, 1989, 1991: chaps. 2–5 and 9, and 1996: chap. 13; McNamara, 1999: chaps. 3–4; Milkis, 1993: chaps. 3–6; Storing, 1995: chaps. 18–22; Tarcov, 1990; Tatalovich and Engeman, 2003.

39. Fairbanks, 1987 and 1993: 53–56; Koritansky, 1999; Melnick, 2000; Rohr, 1995 and 2002; Shulsky, 1991b: chap. 6; Storing and Self, 1963.

40. Most notably the work of John A. Rohr, 1976, 1986, 1989, and 1998; see also Richardson and Nigro, 1987 and 1998.

41. Storing 1964: 46, and see also 1980; Rohr, 1976; Self and Storing, 1963: 212–20.

42. See also Rohr 1986 and 2002; Dannhauser, 1980; Kirwan, 1981; Lawler, Schaefer, and Schaefer, 1998; Maletz, 1991; Melnick, 2000.

43. The quest is for something considerably more than the Senior Executive Service (SES) created by the Civil Service Reform Act of 1978, "which is but a dim shadow of earlier suggested reforms" (Rohr, 1986: 186, and see also ibid.: 39, and 1998: chap. 7, as well as Storing, 1980 and 1995: chap. 15—"Political Parties and the Bureaucracy," and chap. 16—"Leonard D. White and the Study of Public Administration").

44. Connelly, 1994a and 1994b; Landy, 1981; Landy and Levin, 1995; Malbin, 1980 and 1981; Melnick, 1983 and 1994; Strahan, 1990; Wilson and Schramm, 1994; Uhr, 1998.

45. Ceaser, 1979, 1980, and 1981; Diamond, 1992: chap. 11; Mansfield 1965a and b; Milkis, 1993; Storing, 1995: chap. 21; for an analysis of the mutual benefits of the dialectical struggle between party and bureaucratic influence in American government, see Storing, 1995: chap. 15, and Schramm and Wilson, 1993.

46. McWilliams, 1980, 1992, and 2000; see also Goldwin, 1980a and b; Landy, 1993; Milkis, 1999 and 2001.

47. Jaffa 1965: chap. 1; see also Zvesper, 1977.

48. Storing, 1962: chap. 3, and pp. 319, 323, as well as 1995: chaps. 12–13; see also Fairbanks, 1997.

49. Frost, 2003; Marks, 2003; Myers, 2003; Rohr, 1971; Ruderman, 2003.

50. In Storing's words (1981: vol. 1, pp. 6, 71–73), the Anti-Federalists "had *reasons,* and the reasons have weight. They thought—and it cannot easily be denied—that this great national opportunity was profoundly problematical, that it could be neither grasped nor let alone without risking everything. The Anti-Federalists were committed to both union and the states; to both the great American republic and the small, self-governing community; to both commerce and virtue; to both private gain and public good. At its best, Anti-Federalist thought explores these tensions and points to the need for any significant American thought to confront them; for they were not resolved by the Constitution but are inherent in the principles and traditions of American political life." It is true that, in their contest with the Federalists, "they had the weaker argument." But "the Anti-Federalist reservations echo through American history; and it is in the dialogue, not merely in the Federalist victory, that the country's principles are to be discovered." Above all, "the Anti-Federalists could rightly contend that the new Constitution does, after all, depend on something like republican virtue. It is distinguished not by emancipation from this old dependence but by a lack of much attention to the question of how that necessary republican virtue can be maintained. As they took for granted a certain kind of public-spirited leadership, so they took for granted the republican genius of the people; but that cannot prudently be taken for granted. The Federalist solution not only failed to provide for the moral qualities that are necessary to the maintenance of republican government; it tended to undermine them." See also Dry, 1987, 1994, 2003.

51. See also the essays by Engeman, Lawler, McWilliams, and West in Engeman and Zuckert, M., 2004; McWilliams, 1998: 242, highlights those brief but pregnant comments with which Strauss indicated his appreciation of biblical religion's role in American public life. See also Elazar, 1994 and 1998b.

52. Berns, 1984: chaps. 15–17; Brotz, 1970 and 1992; Jaffa, 1965: chap. 7 and 1975; Lerner, 1987: chap. 5; Mansfield, 1991: chap. 7; Marks, 2003; Ruderman, 2002; Schaub, 2000; Storing, 1995: chaps. 7–9 and 11; see also Hinchman and Hinchman, 1998; for explorations of the racial issue as a moral problem in the Founders' thought, see esp. Berns, 1984: chap. 14 and 1987: chap. 1; Goldwin, 1990; Griswold, 1991; Lerner, 1987: chap. 4; Rahe, 1992: Bk. 3, chap. 2; Storing, 1995: chap. 6; Yarbrough, 1991.

53. Ceaser, 1990; Galston, 1987 and 1991; Hennis, 1991; Kessler, 1977; Koritansky, 1986; Kraynak, 1987; Lawler, 1993 and 2004; Maletz, 2001 and 2002; Manent, 1996; Mansfield, 1991: chaps. 13–14; Masugi, 1991; McWilliams, 1992; Salkever, 1990: 245–62; Tessitore, 2002; Thompson, Norma, 2001: chap. 5; Winthrop, 1986 and 1992; Zetterbaum, 1967.

54. Banfield, 1970 and 1974; Brotz, 1980; Clor, 1969 and 1996; Faulkner, 1989; Kessler, 1994; Knippenberg and Lawler, 1996; McDowell and Smith, 1999; McWilliams, 1980, 1987, and 1992; Melzer, Weinberger, and Zinman, 1998 and 2003; Newell, 2002; Schwartz, 2000; Yarbrough, 1998; Wilson, J., 1985a, 1985b, 1993, 1995, and 2002; Winthrop, 1986.

55. Bloom, 1990a, 1990b, 1993, and, above all, Bloom and Jaffa, 1964.

56. Bloom, 1987; the first detailed serious scholarly study of Bloom's argument, its sources, its premises, and its far-reaching implications, is Kinzel, 2002.

57. For good examples, see Brubaker, 1988; Kautz, 1993, 1995, and 1997; Lerner, 1987: chap. 1; Tarcov, 1983a and 1984; Wilson, J., 1985a, 1985b, 1993, 1995, and 2002.

58. See, for example, Elazar, 1996–1998; Glendon, 1987, 1989, and 1991; Kraynak, 2001; Lawler, 1993 and 1999; McWilliams, 1984 and 1987; Owen, 2001; Ruderman and Godwin, 2000.

59. See esp. Bloom, 1987, as well as Baumann, 1990; Ceaser, 1997; Ceaser and McGuinn, 1998; Dannhauser, 1990; Newell, 1990; Schwartz, 1990; Shell, 1990.

60. Scholarship that takes its cue from Strauss has been united, however, in contesting through textual exegesis the historical accuracy, and in deploring some of the overly simplifying civic effects, of the "classical" or "Atlantic" "civic humanist-republican" framework inspired by Hannah Arendt's speculations, elaborated by Pocock,

1975 (for Pocock's expression of indebtedness to Arendt, see 550), and made predominant among historians through the work especially of Bailyn, 1967 and Wood, 1972.

61. For the best articulation, see Diamond, 1992: chap. 21.

62. See Michael Zuckert's discussion (1999) of the evolution of Martin Diamond's judgment on the American regime in light of classical political philosophy; also Zuckert, M., 1990; Forde, 2001; Manent, 1994; Pippin, 1992; Salkever, 1987 and 1990; Tarcov, 1983a. Contrast McWilliams, 1998; Bruell, 1991. Michael Zuckert has recently written (2001) in agreement with Kraynak, 2000: 278–79, that "Mansfield differs from Strauss . . . most strikingly in maintaining, as Kraynak has it, that 'Locke and Madison are modern Aristotelians' . . . [and] that the Lockean theory of rights is better understood in terms of prideful self-assertion than in the Hobbesian terms Strauss attributed to Locke." While this last characterization of the Lockean theory of rights may reflect Zuckert's own view of that theory, I am not convinced that Kraynak has accurately characterized Mansfield's intention—which may be better understood, I believe, as a supplement to, rather than a disagreement with, Strauss's analysis of Locke's Hobbesian core.

63. The problem, if not classical rationalism's way of grappling with it, has become more visible in the work of theologically inspired Straussians (e.g., Lawler, 1999; Manent, 1994) and in the revolution that Meier, 1995, has brought about in the understanding of Carl Schmitt, and the latter's lifelong wrestling, as a political theologian, with Strauss as a political philosopher.

64. All quotations in this and the following paragraph are from LAM, 7–8.

Works Cited

Citations in the text and endnotes from primary sources are by standard pagination, or section numeration, of recognized critical editions. These editions are not listed here, except where peculiarities or page numbers of a specific edition are significant. All translations from primary sources not written in English are my own unless otherwise noted, in which case the full bibliographic citation for the translation used is given below.

Agresto, John (1984) *The Supreme Court and Constitutional Democracy.* Ithaca: Cornell University Press.

Ahrensdorf, Peter (1994) "The Question of Historical Context and the Study of Plato." *Polity* 27: 113–35.

——— (1997) "Thucydides' Realistic Critique of Realism." *Polity* 30: 231–65.

Alvey, James E. (1999) "A Short History of Economics as a Moral Science." *Journal of Markets and Morality* 2 (1): 53–73.

——— (2001) "Adam Smith's Moral Science of Economics." *History of Economics Review* 33: 81–95.

Aron, Raymond (1957) "Introduction" to *Max Weber: Le savant et la politique.* Paris: Plon.

Bailyn, Bernard (1967) *The Ideological Origins of the American Revolution.* Cambridge, Mass.: Harvard University Press.

Banfield, Edward C. (1970) *The Unheavenly City.* Boston: Little, Brown.

——— (1974) *The Unheavenly City Revisited.* Boston: Little, Brown.

———, ed. (1992) *Civility and Citizenship in Liberal Democratic Societies.* New York: Professors World Peace Academy.

Baras, Victor (1975) "Beria's Fall and Ulbricht's Survival." *Soviet Studies* 27 (3): 381–95.

Barber, Sotirios A. (1984) *On What the Constitution Means.* Baltimore: Johns Hopkins University Press.

——— (1986) "Epistemological Skepticism, Hobbesian Natural Right, and Judicial Self-Restraint." *Review of Politics* 48: 374–400.

Bartlett, Robert C. (1994) "The 'Realism' of Classical Political Science." *American Journal of Political Science* 38 (2): 381–402.

——— (1996) "On the Decline of Contemporary Political Developmental Studies." *Review of Politics* 58 (2): 269–98.

——— (2001) *The Idea of Enlightenment: A Post-Mortem Study.* Toronto: University of Toronto Press.

Baumann, Fred (1990) "Historicism and the Constitution." In Bloom, 1990a.

Behnegar, Nasser (1997) "Leo Strauss's Confrontation with Max Weber: A Search for a Genuine Social Science." *Review of Politics* 59 (1): 97–125.

Berlin, Isaiah (1958) *Two Concepts of Liberty.* Oxford: Oxford University Press.

Berns, Walter (1957) *Freedom, Virtue and the First Amendment.* Baton Rouge: Louisiana State University Press.

——— (1962) "Voting Studies." In Storing, 1962.

——— (1976) *The First Amendment and the Future of American Democracy.* New York: Basic Books.

——— (1983a) "Judicial Review and the Rights and the Laws of Nature." *1982 Supreme Court Review:* 49–83.

——— (1983b) "Taking Rights Frivolously." In Douglas MacLean and Claudia Mills, eds., *Liberalism Reconsidered.* Totowa, N.J.: Rowman & Allenheld.

——— (1984) *In Defense of Liberal Democracy.* Chicago: Regnery Gateway.

——— (1987) *Taking the Constitution Seriously.* New York: Simon and Schuster.

——— (2001) *Making Patriots.* Chicago: University of Chicago Press.

Bessette, Joseph M. (1994) *The Mild Voice of Reason: Deliberative Democracy and American National Government.* Chicago: University of Chicago Press.

Bessette, Joseph M., and Tulis, Jeffrey, eds. (1981) *The Presidency in the Constitutional Order.* Baton Rouge: Louisiana State University Press.

Bickel, Alexander (1962) *The Least Dangerous Branch.* Indianapolis: Bobbs-Merrill.

Blais, André (2000) *To Vote or Not to Vote: The Merits and Limits of Rational Choice Theory.* Pittsburgh: University of Pittsburgh Press.

Blitz, Mark (1999) "Government Practice and the School of Strauss."
In Kenneth L. Deutsch and John A. Murley, eds., *Leo Strauss, the
Straussians, and the American Regime.* Lanham, Md.: Rowman &
Littlefield, chap. 29.

Bloom, Allan (1965) *The "Republic" of Plato.* Translated, with an
Interpretive Essay. New York: Basic Books.

———— (1975) "Justice: John Rawls vs. the Tradition of Political
Philosophy." *American Political Science Review* 69 (2): 648–62.

———— (1987) *The Closing of the American Mind: How Higher Education
Has Failed Democracy and Impoverished the Souls of Today's
Students.* New York: Simon and Schuster.

————, ed. (1990a) *Confronting the Constitution: The Challenge to
Locke, Montesquieu, Jefferson, and the Federalists from
Utilitarianism, Historicism, Marxism, Freudianism, Pragmatism,
Existentialism . . .* Washington: AEI Press.

———— (1990b) *Giants and Dwarfs: Essays 1960–1990.* New York:
Simon and Schuster.

———— (1993) *Love and Friendship.* New York: Simon and Schuster.

Bloom, Allan, with Jaffa, Harry V. (1964) *Shakespeare's Politics.* New
York: Basic Books.

Bolotin, David (1979) *Plato's Dialogue on Friendship.* Ithaca: Cornell
University Press.

———— (1987) "Thucydides." In Leo Strauss and Joseph Cropsey, eds.,
History of Political Philosophy, 3rd ed. Chicago: University of
Chicago Press.

———— (1998) *An Approach to Aristotle's Physics: With Particular
Attention to the Role of His Manner of Writing.* Albany: SUNY Press.

Brotz, Howard M. (1970) *The Black Jews of Harlem: Negro Nationalism
and the Dilemmas of Negro Leadership.* New York: Schocken. (Orig.
pub. 1964.)

———— (1974) "Theory and Practice: Ethnomethodology versus
Humane Ethnography." *Jewish Journal of Sociology* 16 (2): 225–36.

———— (1979) "On the History of Sociology." *Jewish Journal of
Sociology* 21 (2): 161–69.

———— (1980) "Multiculturalism in Canada: A Muddle." *Canadian
Public Policy* 6 (1): 41–46.

———— (1992) *African-American Social and Political Thought, 1850–*

1920. New Brunswick, N.J.: Transaction Publishers. (Orig. pub. 1966.)

Brubaker, Stanley C. (1985a) "Reconsidering Dworkin's Case for Judicial Activism." *Journal of Politics* 46 (4): 503–19.

——— (1985b) Review of Sotirios Barber, *On What the Constitution Means. Constitutional Commentary* 2: 261–76.

——— (1985c) "Taking Dworkin Seriously." *Review of Politics* 47: 45–65.

——— (1988) "Can Liberals Punish?" *American Political Science Review* 82 (3): 821–36.

——— (1998) "The Court as Astigmatic Schoolmarm: A Case for the Clear-Sighted Citizen." In Bradford P. Wilson and Ken Masugi, eds., *The Supreme Court and American Constitutionalism.* Lanham, Md.: Rowman & Littlefield.

Brubaker, Stanley C., and Barber, Sotirios (1987) "Republican Government and Judicial Restraint." *Review of Politics* 49 (4): 570–73.

Bruell, Christopher (1974) "Thucydides' View of Athenian Imperialism." *American Political Science Review* 68 (1): 11–17.

——— (1991) "A Return to Classical Political Philosophy and the Understanding of the American Founding." *Review of Politics* 53 (1): 173–86.

——— (1994) "On Plato's Political Philosophy." *Review of Politics* 56: 261–82.

——— (1999) *On the Socratic Education: An Introduction to the Shorter Platonic Dialogues.* Lanham, Md.: Rowman & Littlefield.

Burns, Timothy (1994) *After History? Francis Fukuyama and His Critics.* Lanham, Md.: Rowman & Littlefield.

Busch, Nathan (2004) *No End in Sight: The Continuing Menace of Nuclear Proliferation.* Lexington: University Press of Kentucky.

Canavan, Francis (1971) "Freedom of Speech and Press: For What Purpose?" *American Journal of Jurisprudence* 16 (1): 95–142.

——— (1995) *The Political Economy of Edmund Burke: The Role of Property in His Thought.* New York: Fordham University Press.

Cantor, Paul (1991) "Leo Strauss and Contemporary Hermeneutics." In Alan Udoff, ed., *Leo Strauss's Thought: Toward a Critical Engagement.* Boulder, Colo.: Lynne Rienner.

Cassin, René (1972) *La Pensée et l'action.* Paris: F. Lalov.

Ceaser, James W. (1979) *Presidential Selection: Theory and Development.* Princeton: Princeton University Press.

———— (1980) "Political Change and Party Reform." In Goldwin, 1980b.

———— (1981) "Direct Participation in Politics." *Proceedings of the American Academy of Political Science* 34 (2): 121–37.

———— (1990) *Liberal Democracy and Political Science.* Baltimore: Johns Hopkins University Press.

———— (1997) *Reconstructing America: The Symbol of America in Modern Thought.* New Haven: Yale University Press.

Ceaser, James W., and McGuinn, Patrick J. (1998) "Civic Education Reconsidered." *Public Interest* (133): 84–103.

Clor, Harry M. (1969) *Obscenity and Public Morality: Censorship in a Liberal Society.* Chicago: University of Chicago Press.

————, ed. (1971) *Censorship and Freedom of Expression.* Chicago: Rand McNally.

———— (1996) *Public Morality and Liberal Society: Essays on Decency, Law, and Pornography.* Notre Dame: University of Notre Dame Press.

Collingwood, R. G. (1970) *An Autobiography.* Oxford: Oxford University Press.

Connelly, William F., Jr. (1994a) "Congress: Representation and Deliberation." In Peter Lawler and Roberta Schaefer, eds., *The American Experiment: Essays on the Theory and Practice of Liberty.* Lanham, Md.: Rowman & Littlefield.

———— (1994b) *Congress's Permanent Minority? Republicans in the U.S. House.* Lanham, Md.: Rowman & Littlefield.

Corwin, Edward S. (1940) *The President: Office and Powers.* New York: New York University Press.

Croly, Herbert (1915) *Progressive Democracy.* New York: Macmillan.

Cronin, Thomas, ed. (1989) *Inventing the American Presidency.* Lawrence: University Press of Kansas.

Cropsey, Joseph (1957) *Polity and Economy: An Interpretation of the Principles of Adam Smith.* The Hague: Martinus Nijhoff.

———— (1977) "What Is Welfare Economics?" In *Political Philosophy and the Issues of Politics.* Chicago: University of Chicago Press.

Crovitz, L. Gordon, and Rabkin, Jeremy, eds. (1989) *The Fettered Presidency.* Washington: AEI Press.

Danford, John (1978) *Wittgenstein and Political Philosophy: A Reexamination of the Foundations of Social Science.* Chicago: University of Chicago Press.

———— (1980) "Adam Smith, Equality, and the Wealth of Sympathy." *American Journal of Political Science* 24 (4): 674–95.

———— (1990) *David Hume and the Problem of Reason: Recovering the Human Sciences.* New Haven: Yale University Press.

Dannhauser, Werner (1980) "Reflections on Statesmanship and Bureaucracy." In Robert A. Goldwin, ed., *Bureaucrats, Policy Analysts, Statesmen: Who Leads?* Washington: AEI Press.

———— (1990) "Existentialism and Democracy." In Bloom, 1990a.

Dewey, John (1939) *Freedom and Culture.* New York: G. P. Putnam's Sons.

———— (1942) *German Philosophy and Politics,* rev. ed. New York: G. P. Putnam's Sons.

Diamond, Martin (1992) *As Far as Republican Principles Will Admit.* Ed. William Schambra. Washington: AEI Press.

Dobbs, Darrell (1987) "Reckless Rationalism and Heroic Reverence in Homer's *Odyssey*." *American Political Science Review* 81: 491–508.

Dobbs, Darrell, and Grafstein, Robert (1988) "Rationalism or Revelation?" *American Political Science Review* 82: 579–87.

Dry, Murray (1985) "Federalism and the Constitution: The Founders' Design and Contemporary Constitutional Law." *Constitutional Commentary* 2: 233–50.

———— (1987) "The Case against Ratification: Anti-Federalist Constitutional Thought." In Leonard W. Levy and Dennis J. Mahoney, eds., *The Framing and Ratification of the Constitution.* New York: Macmillan.

———— (1994) "The Constitutional Thought of the Anti-Federalists." In Peter Augustine Lawler and Robert Martin Schaefer, eds., *The American Experiment: Essays on the Theory and Practice of Liberty.* Lanham, Md.: Rowman & Littlefield.

———— (2003) "Anti-Federalist Political Thought: Brutus and Federal Farmer." In Frost and Sikkenga, 2003.

Eden, Robert (1987) "Weber and Nietzsche: Liberating the Social Sciences from Historicism." In Wolfgang J. Mommsen et al., eds., *Max Weber and His Contemporaries.* London: Allen and Unwin.

Elazar, Daniel J. (1990) *Constitutionalism: The Israeli and American Experiences.* Lanham, Md.: University Press of America.

——— (1994) *Covenant in the Nineteenth Century: The Decline of an American Political Tradition.* Lanham, Md.: Rowman & Littlefield.

——— (1996–1998) *The Covenant Tradition in Politics.* 4 vols. New Brunswick, N.J.: Transaction Publishers.

——— (1998a) *Constitutionalizing Globalization: The Postmodern Revival of Confederal Arrangements.* Lanham, Md.: Rowman & Littlefield.

——— (1998b) *Covenant and Civil Society: The Constitutional Matrix of Modern Democracy.* New Brunswick, N.J.: Transaction.

Engeman, Thomas S., and Zuckert, Michael P., eds. (2004) *Protestantism and the American Founding.* Notre Dame: University of Notre Dame Press.

Epstein, David (1984) *The Political Theory of the Federalist.* Chicago: University of Chicago Press.

Fairbanks, Charles H., Jr. (1987) "Bureaucratic Politics in the Soviet Union and in the Ottoman Empire." *Comparative Strategy* 6 (3): 333–62.

——— (1993) "The Nature of the Beast." *National Interest* 31: 46–56.

——— (1995a) "The Postcommunist Wars." *Journal of Democracy* 6 (4): 18–34.

——— (1995b) "A Tired Anarchy." *National Interest* 39: 15–25.

——— (1997) "The Public Void: Antipolitics in the Former Soviet Union." In Andreas Schedler, ed., *The End of Politics? Explorations into Modern Antipolitics.* New York: St. Martin's.

Faulkner, Robert K. (1968) *The Jurisprudence of John Marshall.* Princeton: Princeton University Press.

——— (1978) "Bickel's Constitution: The Problem of Moderate Liberalism." *American Political Science Review* 72: 925–40.

——— (1989) "Difficulties of Equal Dignity: The Court and the Family." In Robert A. Goldwin and William A. Schambra, eds., *The Constitution, the Courts, and the Quest for Justice.* Washington: AEI Press.

——— (1990) "Liberal Plans for the World: Locke, Kant, and World Ecology Theories." *International Journal on World Peace* 7: 61–86.

Flaumenhaft, Harvey (1992) *The Effective Republic: Administration and the Constitution in the Thought of Alexander Hamilton.* Durham, N.C.: Duke University Press.

Forbes, H. D. (1985) *Nationalism, Ethnocentrism, and Personality: Social Science and Critical Theory.* Chicago: University of Chicago Press.

———— (1997) *Ethnic Conflict: Commerce, Culture, and the Contact Hypothesis.* New Haven: Yale University Press.

———— (2004) "Positive Political Theory." In Gerald F. Gaus and Chandran Kukathas, eds., *Handbook of Political Theory.* London: Sage Publications.

Forde, Steven (1989) *The Ambition to Rule: Alcibiades and the Politics of Imperialism in Athens.* Ithaca: Cornell University Press.

———— (1992a) "Benjamin Franklin's *Autobiography* and the Education of America." *American Political Science Review* 86: 357–68.

———— (1992b) "Classical Realism." In Terry Nardin and David Mapel, eds., *Traditions of International Ethics.* Cambridge: Cambridge University Press.

———— (1995) "International Realism: Thucydides, Machiavelli, and Neorealism." *International Studies Quarterly* 39 (2): 141–60.

———— (1998) "Hugo Grotius' Approach on Ethics and War." *American Political Science Review* 92 (3): 639–48.

———— (2001) "Natural Law, Theology, and Morality in Locke." *American Journal of Political Science* 45 (2): 396–409.

Frachon, Alain, and Vernet, Daniel (2004) *L'Amérique messianique: Les Guerres des néo-conservateurs.* Paris: Seuil.

Franklin, Benjamin (1959–) *Papers.* Ed. Leonard W. Labaree et al. New Haven: Yale University Press.

Frisch, Morton J. (1978) "Hamilton's Report on Manufactures and Political Philosophy." *Publius: The Journal of Federalism* 8 (3): 129–39.

Frisch, Morton J., and Stevens, Richard G., eds. (1971) *American Political Thought: The Philosophic Dimensions of American Statesmanship.* New York: Charles Scribner's Sons.

Frost, Bryan-Paul (1996) "Raymond Aron's *Peace and War,* Thirty Years Later." *International Journal* 51: 339–61.

———— (1997) "Resurrecting a Neglected Theorist: The Philosophical

Foundations of Raymond Aron's Theory of International Relations." *Review of International Studies* 23: 143–66.

——— (1999) "A Critical Introduction to Alexandre Kojève's *Esquisse d'une phénomenologie du droit*." *Review of Metaphysics* 52: 595–640.

——— (2003) "Religion, Nature, and Disobedience in the Thought of Ralph Waldo Emerson and Henry David Thoreau." In Frost and Sikkenga, 2003.

Frost, Bryan-Paul, and Sikkenga, Jeffrey, eds. (2003) *History of American Political Thought*. Lanham, Md.: Lexington Books.

Fukuyama, Francis (1989) "The End of History." *National Interest* 16: 3–18.

——— (1992) *The End of History and the Last Man*. New York: Free Press.

Galston, William (1987) "Tocqueville on Liberalism and Religion." *Social Research* 54 (3): 499–518.

——— (1991) *Liberal Purposes: Goods, Virtue, and Diversity in the Liberal State*. Cambridge: Cambridge University Press.

Glendon, Mary Ann (1987) *Abortion and Divorce in Western Law: American Failures, European Challenges*. Cambridge, Mass.: Harvard University Press.

——— (1989) *The Transformation of Family Law: State, Law, and Family in the United States and Western Europe*. Chicago: University of Chicago Press.

——— (1991) *Rights Talk: The Impoverishment of Political Discourse*. New York: Free Press.

Glenn, Gary D. (1999) "Walter Berns: The Constitution and American Liberal Democracy." In Kenneth L. Deutsch and John A. Murley, eds., *Leo Strauss, the Straussians, and the American Regime*. Lanham, Md.: Rowman & Littlefield.

Goldstein, Leslie Friedman (1991) *In Defense of the Text: Democracy and Constitutional Theory*. Savage, Md.: Rowman & Littlefield.

——— (1992) *Feminist Jurisprudence: The Difference Debate*. Lanham, Md.: Rowman & Littlefield.

——— (2001) *Constituting Federal Sovereignty: The European Union in Comparative Perspective*. Baltimore: Johns Hopkins University Press.

Goldwin, Robert A., ed. (1980a) *How Democratic Is the Constitution?* Washington: AEI Press.

———, ed. (1980b) *Political Parties in the Eighties*. Washington: AEI Press.

——— (1990) *Why Blacks, Women, and Jews Are Not Mentioned in the Constitution*. Washington: AEI Press.

——— (1997) *From Parchment to Power: How James Madison Used the Bill of Rights to Save the Constitution*. Washington: AEI Press.

Goldwin, Robert A., and Kaufman, Arthur, eds. (1988) *Constitution Makers on Constitution Making: The Experience of Eight Nations*. Washington: AEI Press.

——— eds. (1989) *Forging Unity Out of Diversity: The Approaches of Eight Nations*. Washington: AEI Press.

Goldwin, Robert A., and Licht, Robert A., eds. (1990) *Foreign Policy and the Constitution*. Washington: AEI Press.

Goldwin, Robert A., and Schambra, William, A., eds. (1982) *How Capitalistic Is the Constitution?* Washington: AEI Press.

Greenstein, Fred I. (1978) "Change and Continuity in the Modern Presidency." In Anthony King, ed., *The New American Political System*. Washington: AEI Press.

Greenstein, Fred I., Berman, Larry, and Felzenberg, Alvin S. (1977) *Evolution of the Modern Presidency: A Bibliographical Survey*. Washington: AEI Press.

Grey, Thomas (1975) "Do We Have an Unwritten Constitution?" *Stanford Law Review* 27: 703–48.

Griswold, Charles (1991) "Rights and Wrongs: Jefferson, Slavery, and Philosophical Quandaries." In Michael J. Lacey and Knud Haakonssen, eds., *A Culture of Rights*. Cambridge: Cambridge University Press.

——— (1998) *Adam Smith and the Virtues of Enlightenment*. Cambridge: Cambridge University Press.

Hamburger, Joseph (1990) "Utilitarianism." In Bloom, 1990a.

Hassner, Pierre (1961) "Les concepts de guerre et de paix chez Kant." *Revue française de science politique* 11 (3): 642–70.

——— (1995) *La violence et la paix: De la bombe atomique au nettoyage ethnique*. Paris: Editions Esprit.

——— (1997) "Rousseau and the Theory and Practice of International Relations." In Clifford Orwin and Nathan Tarcov, eds., *The Legacy of Rousseau*. Chicago: University of Chicago Press.

———— (2003) *La terreur et l'empire: La violence et la paix II.* Paris: Le Seuil.

Hassner, Pierre, and Vaïsse, Justin (2003) *Washington et le monde: Dilemmes d'une superpuissance.* Paris: Autremont.

Hennis, Wilhelm (1963) *Politik und praktische Philosophie: Eine Studie zur Rekonstruction der politischen Wissenschaft.* Neuwied: Luchterhand.

———— (1991) "In Search of the 'New Science of Politics.'" In Masugi, 1991.

Hinchman, Lewis P., and Hinchman, Sandra K. (1998) "Australia's Judicial Revolution: Aboriginal Land Rights and the Transformation of Liberalism." *Polity* 31: 23–51.

Horelick, Arnold L., and Rush, Myron (1966) *Strategic Power and Soviet Foreign Policy.* Chicago: University of Chicago Press.

Horwitz, Robert H., ed. (1986) *The Moral Foundations of the American Republic,* 3rd ed. Charlottesville: University Press of Virginia.

Jacobsohn, Gary (1977) *Pragmatism, Statesmanship, and the Supreme Court.* Ithaca: Cornell University Press.

———— (1983) *Apple of Gold: Constitutionalism in Israel and the United States.* Princeton: Princeton University Press.

———— (1986) *The Supreme Court and the Decline of Constitutional Aspiration.* Totowa, N.J.: Rowman & Littlefield.

———— (2003) *The Wheel of Law: India's Secularism in Comparative Constitutional Context.* Princeton: Princeton University Press.

Jaffa, Harry V. (1959) *Crisis of the House Divided: An Interpretation of the Issues in the Lincoln-Douglas Debates.* Garden City, N.Y.: Doubleday.

———— (1965) *Equality and Liberty: Theory and Practice in American Politics.* Oxford: Oxford University Press.

———— (1975) "Reflections on Thoreau and Lincoln: Civil Disobedience and the American Tradition." In *The Conditions of Freedom: Essays in Political Philosophy.* Baltimore: Johns Hopkins University Press.

Jefferson, Thomas (1984) *Writings.* New York: Library of America.

Johnson, Laurie M. (1993) *Thucydides, Hobbes, and the Interpretation of Realism.* DeKalb, Ill.: Northern Illinois University Press.

Kautz, Steven (1993) "Liberalism and the Idea of Toleration." *American Journal of Political Science* 37 (2): 610–32.

———— (1995) *Liberalism and Community.* Ithaca: Cornell University Press.

———— (1997) "Privacy and Community." In Clifford Orwin and Nathan Tarcov, eds., *The Legacy of Rousseau.* Chicago: University of Chicago Press.

———— (2003) "Abraham Lincoln: The Moderation of a Democratic Statesman." In Frost and Sikkenga, 2003.

Kessler, Sanford (1977) "Tocqueville on Civil Religion and Liberal Democracy." *Journal of Politics* 39: 119–46.

———— (1994) *Tocqueville's Civil Religion.* Albany: SUNY Press.

————, ed. (2000) *Democracy in America,* by Alexis de Tocqueville. Trans. Stephen Grant. Indianapolis: Hackett.

Kinzel, Till (2002) *Platonische Kulturkritik in Amerika: Studien zu Allan Blooms "The Closing of the American Mind."* Berlin: Duncker and Humblot.

Kirwan, Kent A. (1981) "Herbert J. Storing and the Study of Public Administration." *Political Science Reviewer* 11: 193–222.

Knippenberg, Joseph (1989) "Moving beyond Fear: Rousseau and Kant on Cosmopolitan Education." *Journal of Politics* 51 (4): 809–27.

Knippenberg, Joseph, and Lawler, Peter, eds. (1996) *Poets, Princes, and Private Citizens: Literary Alternatives to Postmodern Politics.* Lanham, Md.: Rowman & Littlefield.

Koritansky, John (1986) *Alexis de Tocqueville and the New Science of Politics: An Interpretation of Democracy in America.* Durham, N.C.: Carolina Academic Press.

———— (1999) *Public Administration in the United States.* Newburyport, Mass.: Focus Publishing.

Krause, Sharon (2002) *Liberalism with Honor.* Cambridge, Mass.: Harvard University Press.

Kraynak, Robert P. (1987) "Tocqueville's Constitutionalism." *American Political Science Review* 81 (4): 1175–95.

———— (2000) "The Care of Souls in a Constitutional Democracy: Some Lessons from Harvey Mansfield and Alexander Solzhenitsyn." In Mark Blitz and William Kristol, eds., *Educating the Prince: Essays in Honor of Harvey Mansfield.* Lanham, Md.: Rowman & Littlefield.

———— (2001) *Christian Faith and Modern Democracy: God and Politics in the Fallen World.* Notre Dame: University of Notre Dame Press.

Kurland, Philip B., and Lerner, Ralph, eds. (1986) *The Founders' Constitution.* 5 vols. Chicago: University of Chicago Press.

Landy, Marc (1981) "Policy Analysis as a Vocation." *World Politics* 33: 468–84.

———— (1993) "Public Policy and Citizenship." In Helen Ingram and Steven Rathgeb Smith, eds., *Public Policy for Democracy.* Washington: Brookings Institution.

Landy, Marc, and Levin, Martin, eds. (1995) *The New Politics of Public Policy.* Baltimore: Johns Hopkins University Press.

Landy, Marc, and Milkis, Sidney M. (2000) *Presidential Greatness.* Lawrence: University Press of Kansas.

Lawler, Peter Augustine (1993) *The Restless Mind: Alexis De Tocqueville on the Origin and Perpetuation of Human Liberty.* Lanham, Md.: Rowman & Littlefield.

———— (1999) *Postmodernism Rightly Understood: The Return to Realism in American Thought.* Lanham, Md.: Rowman & Littlefield.

————, ed. (2004) *Democracy and Its Friendly Critics: Tocqueville and Political Life Today.* Lanham, Md.: Lexington Books.

Lawler, Peter Augustine, Schaefer, Roberta, and Schaefer, David, eds. (1998) *Active Duty: Administration as Democratic Statesmanship.* Lanham, Md.: Rowman & Littlefield.

Lee, Ronald C. (2002) "Justifying Empire: Pericles, Polk, and a Dilemma of Democratic Leadership." *Polity* 34: 503–31.

Lerner, Ralph (1979) "Commerce and Character: The Anglo-American as New-Model Man." *William and Mary Quarterly,* 3rd series, 36: 3–26.

———— (1987) *The Thinking Revolutionary: Principle and Practice in the New Republic.* Ithaca: Cornell University Press.

Lindholm, Tore (1992) "Article 1." In Asbjørn Eide et al., eds., *The Universal Declaration of Human Rights: A Commentary.* Oslo: Scandinavian University Press.

Lindsay, Thomas (1991) "James Madison on Religion and Politics: Rhetoric and Reality." *American Political Science Review* 85: 1321–37.

Lord, Carnes (1988) *The Presidency and the Management of National Security.* New York: Free Press.

————— (2003) *The Modern Prince: What Leaders Need to Know Now.* New Haven: Yale University Press.

Macpherson, C. B. (1962) *The Political Theory of Possessive Individualism: Hobbes to Locke.* Oxford: Oxford University Press.

————— (1972) "Hobbes's Bourgeois Man." In *Democratic Theory: Essays in Retrieval.* Oxford: Oxford University Press.

Mahoney, Daniel J. (1992) *The Liberal Political Science of Raymond Aron: A Critical Introduction.* Lanham, Md.: Rowman & Littlefield.

————— (1996) *DeGaulle: Statesmanship, Grandeur, and Modern Democracy.* Westport, Conn.: Praeger.

Malbin, Michael (1980) *Unelected Representatives: Congressional Staff and the Future of Representative Government.* New York: Basic Books.

————— (1981) *Religion and Politics: The Intention of the Authors of the First Amendment.* Washington: AEI Press.

Maletz, Donald J. (1991) "The Place of Constitutionalism in the Education of Public Administrators." *Administration and Society* 23 (3): 374–94.

————— (2001) "Tocqueville on the Society of Liberties." *Review of Politics* 63: 461–83.

————— (2002) "Tocqueville's Tyranny of the Majority Reconsidered." *Journal of Politics* 64: 741–63.

Manent, Pierre (1994) *La cité de l'homme.* Paris: Fayard.

————— (1996) *Tocqueville and the Nature of Democracy.* Trans. John Waggoner. Lanham, Md.: Rowman & Littlefield.

————— (1998) *Modern Liberty and Its Discontents.* Ed. and trans. Daniel J. Mahoney and Paul Seaton. Lanham, Md.: Rowman & Littlefield.

Mansfield, Harvey C. (1964) "Party Government and the Settlement of 1688." *American Political Science Review* 58 (3): 933–46.

————— (1965a) *Statesmanship and Party Government.* Chicago: University of Chicago Press.

————— (1965b) "Whether Party Government Is Inevitable." *Political Science Quarterly* 80 (2): 517–42.

————— (1968) "Modern and Medieval Representation." *Nomos* 11: 55–82.

————— (1971) "Hobbes and the Science of Indirect Government." *American Political Science Review* 65 (1): 97–110.

——— (1978) *The Spirit of Liberalism.* Cambridge, Mass.: Harvard University Press.

——— (1979) "On the Political Character of Property in Locke." In A. Kontos, ed., *Powers, Possessions, and Freedom: Essays in Honour of C. B. Macpherson.* Toronto: University of Toronto Press.

——— (1981) "Machiavelli's Political Science." *American Political Science Review* 75 (1): 293–305.

——— (1989) *Taming the Prince.* New York: Free Press.

——— (1990) "Social Science and the Constitution." In Bloom, 1990a.

——— (1991) *America's Constitutional Soul.* Baltimore: Johns Hopkins University Press.

——— (1996) *Machiavelli's Virtue.* Chicago: University of Chicago Press.

Mansfield, Harvey C., and Winthrop, Delba, eds. and trans. (2000) *Democracy in America,* by Alexis de Tocqueville. Chicago: University of Chicago Press.

Maritain, Jacques (1950) "Introduction." *Human Rights: Comments and Interpretations: A Symposium Edited by UNESCO.* London: Allan Wingate.

Marks, Jonathan (2003) "Co-workers in the Kingdom of Culture: W. E. B. Du Bois's Vision of Race Synthesis." In Frost and Sikkenga, 2003.

Masugi, Ken, ed. (1991) *Interpreting Tocqueville's Democracy in America.* Lanham, Md.: Rowman & Littlefield.

McDowell, Gary, ed. (1981) *Taking the Constitution Seriously: Essays on the Constitution and Constitutional Law.* Dubuque, Iowa: Kendall/Hunt.

——— (1982) *Equity and the Constitution: The Supreme Court, Equitable Relief, and Public Policy.* Chicago: University of Chicago Press.

——— (1998) "The Language of Law and the Foundations of American Constitutionalism." *William and Mary Quarterly,* 3rd series, 55: 375–98.

McDowell, Gary, and Noble, Sharon L., eds. (1997) *Reason and Republicanism: Thomas Jefferson's Legacy of Liberty.* Lanham, Md.: Rowman & Littlefield.

McDowell, Gary, and Smith, Jinney S., eds. (1999) *Juvenile Delinquency in the United States and the United Kingdom.* New York: St. Martin's Press.

McNamara, Peter (1998) *Political Economy and Statesmanship: Adam Smith and Alexander Hamilton on the Foundation of the Commercial Republic.* DeKalb, Ill.: Northern Illinois University Press.

———, ed. (1999) *The Noblest Minds: Fame, Honor, and the American Founding.* Lanham, Md.: Rowman & Littlefield.

McWilliams, Wilson Carey (1980) "Parties as Civic Associations." In Gerald Pomper, ed., *Party Renewal in America: Theory and Practice.* New York: Praeger.

——— (1983) "In Good Faith: On the Foundations of American Politics." *Humanities in Society* 6: 19–40.

——— (1984) "The Bible in the American Tradition." In M. J. Aronoff, ed., *Religion and Politics (Political Anthropology III).* New Brunswick, N.J.: Transaction Books.

——— (1987) "Civil Religion in the Age of Reason: Thomas Paine on Liberalism, Redemption, and Revolution." *Social Research* 54 (3): 447–90.

——— (1992) "Tocqueville and Responsible Parties: Individualism, Participation, and Citizenship in America." In John K. White and Jerome Mileur, eds., *Challenges to Party Government.* Carbondale, Ill.: Southern Illinois University Press.

——— (1998) "Leo Strauss and the Dignity of American Political Thought." *Review of Politics* 60 (2): 231–46.

——— (2000) *Beyond the Politics of Disappointment?* Chatham, N.J.: Chatham House.

Meier, Heinrich (1995) *Carl Schmitt and Leo Strauss: The Hidden Dialogue.* Trans. J. Harvey Lomax. Chicago: University of Chicago Press.

——— (2005a) "How Strauss Became Strauss." In Svetozar Minkov and Stéphane Douard, eds., *Enlightening Revolutions: Essays in Honor of Ralph Lerner.* Lanham, Md.: Lexington Books.

——— (2005b) *Leo Strauss and the Theologico-Political Problem.* Cambridge: Cambridge University Press.

Melnick, R. Shep (1983) *Regulation and the Courts: The Case of the Clean Air Act.* Washington: Brookings Institution.

——— (1994) *Between the Lines: Interpreting Welfare Rights.* Washington: Brookings Institution.

———— (2000) "Constitutional Bureaucracy." In Mark Blitz and William Kristol, eds., *Educating the Prince: Essays in Honor of Harvey Mansfield.* Lanham, Md.: Rowman & Littlefield.

Melzer, Arthur, Weinberger, Jerry, and Zinman, M. Richard, eds. (1998) *Multiculturalism and American Democracy.* Lawrence: University Press of Kansas.

————, eds. (2003) *The Public Intellectual: Between Philosophy and Politics.* Lanham, Md.: Rowman & Littlefield.

Milkis, Sidney M. (1993) *The President and the Parties: The Transformation of the American Party System since the New Deal.* New York: Oxford University Press.

———— (1999) *Political Parties and Constitutional Government: Remaking American Democracy.* Baltimore: Johns Hopkins University Press.

———— (2001) "Political Parties, the Constitution, and Popular Sovereignty." In Peter Bathory and Nancy Schwartz, eds., *Friends and Citizens: Essays in Honor of Wilson Carey McWilliams.* Lanham, Md.: Rowman & Littlefield.

Miller, Eugene F. (1971) "David Easton's Political Theory." *Political Science Reviewer* 1: 184–235.

———— (1972) "Positivism, Historicism, and Political Inquiry." *American Political Science Review* 66: 3.

———— (1999) "Leo Strauss: Philosophy and American Social Science." In Kenneth L. Deutsch and John A. Murley, eds., *Leo Strauss, the Straussians, and the American Regime.* Lanham, Md.: Rowman & Littlefield.

Minowitz, Peter (1993a) "Machiavellianism Come of Age? Leo Strauss on Modernity and Economics." *Political Science Reviewer* 22: 157–97.

———— (1993b) *Profits, Priests, and Princes: Adam Smith's Emancipation of Economics from Politics and Religion.* Stanford: Stanford University Press.

Morgenthau, Hans J. (1958) *Dilemmas of Politics.* Chicago: University of Chicago Press.

———— (1978) *Politics among Nations,* 5th ed. New York: Alfred A. Knopf.

Morsink, Johannes (1999) *The Universal Declaration of Human Rights:*

Origins, Drafting, and Intent. Philadelphia: University of
    Pennsylvania Press.

Myers, Peter C. (2003) "The Two Revolutions of Martin Luther
    King, Jr." In Frost and Sikkenga, 2003.

Neustadt, Richard (1980) *Presidential Power,* 3rd ed. New York: John
    Wiley & Sons. (Orig. pub. 1960.)

Newell, Waller R. (1987) "How Original Is Machiavelli?
    A Consideration of Skinner's Interpretation of Virtue and
    Fortune." *Political Theory* 15: 612–34.

——— (1990) "Reflections on Marxism and America." In Bloom,
    1990a.

——— (2002) *The Search for the Manly Heart: Love, Courage, Pride,
    Family, Country.* New York: Regan Books/HarperCollins.

Nichols, David K. (1994) *The Myth of the Modern Presidency.* University
    Park: Pennsylvania State University Press.

Nichols, James H., Jr. (1990) "Pragmatism and the U.S. Constitution."
    In Bloom, 1990a.

Nichols, James H., Jr., and Wright, Colin, eds. (1990) *From Political
    Economy to Economics—and Back?* San Francisco: Institute for
    Contemporary Studies.

Orwin, Clifford (1994) *The Humanity of Thucydides.* Princeton:
    Princeton University Press.

——— (1996) "Distant Compassion: CNN and Borrioboola-Gha."
    National Interest 43: 42–49.

——— (2000) "Compassion and the Softening of Mores." *Journal of
    Democracy* 11: 142–48.

Orwin, Clifford, and Stoner, James R., Jr. (1990)
    "Neoconstitutionalism? Rawls, Dworkin, and Nozick." In Bloom,
    1990a.

Owen, J. Judd (2001) *Religion and the Demise of Liberal Rationalism:
    The Foundational Crisis of the Separation of Church and State.*
    Chicago: University of Chicago Press.

Palmer, Michael (1992) *Love of Glory and the Common Good: Aspects of
    the Political Thought of Thucydides.* Lanham, Md.: Rowman &
    Littlefield.

Pangle, Thomas, and Ahrensdorf, Peter (1999) *Justice among Nations:
    On the Moral Basis of Power and Peace.* Lawrence: University Press
    of Kansas.

Paynter, John E. (1996) "The Rhetorical Design of John Adams's *Defense of the Constitutions of . . . America.*" *Review of Politics* 58: 531–60.

Pippin, Robert (1992) "The Modern World of Leo Strauss." *Political Theory* 20 (3): 448–72.

Plattner, Marc F. (1982) "American Democracy and the Acquisitive Spirit." In Robert A. Goldwin and William A. Schambra, eds., *How Capitalistic Is the Constitution?* Washington: AEI Press.

———, ed. (1984) *Human Rights in Our Time.* Boulder, Colo.: Westview Press.

——— (1990) "Capitalism." In Bloom, 1990a.

——— (2002) "Globalization and Self-Government." *Journal of Democracy* 13 (3): 54–67.

Pocock, J. G. A. (1975) *The Machiavellian Moment: Florentine Political Thought and the Atlantic Republican Tradition.* Princeton: Princeton University Press.

Rabkin, Jeremy (1989) *Judicial Compulsions: How Public Law Distorts Public Policy.* New York: Basic Books.

——— (1997) "Grotius, Vattel and Locke: An Older View of Liberalism and Nationality." *Review of Politics* 59 (2): 293–322.

——— (1998a) "American Constitutional Sovereignty vs. International Law: Where Is the Supreme Court?" In Bradford P. Wilson and Ken Masugi, eds., *The Supreme Court and American Constitutionalism.* Lanham, Md.: Rowman & Littlefield.

——— (1998b) *Why Sovereignty Matters.* Washington: AEI Press.

——— (2005) *Law without Nations? Why Constitutional Government Requires Sovereign States.* Princeton: Princeton University Press.

Rahe, Paul A. (1992) *Republics Ancient and Modern: Classical Republicanism and the American Revolution.* Chapel Hill: University of North Carolina Press.

——— (2000) "Situating Machiavelli." In James Hankins, ed., *Renaissance Civic Humanism.* Cambridge: Cambridge University Press.

———, ed. (2005) *Machiavelli's Liberal Republican Legacy.* Cambridge: Cambridge University Press.

Rawls, John (1971) *A Theory of Justice.* Cambridge, Mass.: Harvard University Press.

———— (1985) "Justice as Fairness: Political not Metaphysical." *Philosophy and Public Affairs* 14: 223–51.

Rhoads, Steven E. (1980) "How Much Should We Spend to Save a Life?" In Rhoads, ed., *Valuing Life: Public Policy Dilemmas.* Boulder, Colo.: Westview Press.

———— (1985) *The Economist's View of the World: Government, Markets, and Public Policy.* Cambridge: Cambridge University Press.

———— (1993) *Incomparable Worth: Pay Equity Meets the Market.* Cambridge: Cambridge University Press.

Richardson, William D., and Nigro, Lloyd G. (1987) "Self-Interest Properly Understood: The American Character and Public Administration," *Administration and Society* 19 (2): 157–177.

———— (1998) "Citizen Character and Public Administration in the American Regime: Connecting 1787 and 1887." *Administration Theory & Praxis* 20 (1): 32–42.

Riker, William H. (1991a) "Response to Tulis." *Studies in American Political Development* 5: 293–300.

———— (1991b) "Why Negative Campaigning Is Rational: The Rhetoric of the Ratification Campaign of 1787–88." *Studies in American Political Development* 5: 224–83.

Rohr, John A. (1971) *Prophets without Honor: Public Policy and the Selective Conscientious Objector.* Nashville, Tenn.: Abingdon.

———— (1976) "The Study of Ethics in the Public Administration Curriculum." *Public Administration Review* 10: 398–406.

———— (1986) *To Run a Constitution: The Legitimacy of the Administrative State.* Lawrence: University Press of Kansas.

———— (1989) *Ethics for Bureaucrats: An Essay on Law and Values,* 2nd ed., revised and expanded (Foreword by Herbert J. Storing). New York: Marcel Dekker.

———— (1990) "Ethics in Public Administration: A 'State of the Discipline' Report." In Naomi B. Lynn and Aaron Wildavsky, eds., *Public Administration: The State of the Discipline.* Chatham, N.J.: Chatham House.

———— (1995) *Founding Republics in France and America: A Study in Constitutional Governance.* Lawrence: University Press of Kansas.

———— (1998) *Public Service, Ethics, and Constitutional Practice.* Lawrence: University Press of Kansas.

———— (2002) *Civil Servants and Their Constitutions.* Lawrence: University Press of Kansas.

Rorty, Richard (1989) *Contingency, Irony, and Solidarity.* Cambridge: Cambridge University Press.

———— (1991) *Objectivity, Relativism, and Truth.* Cambridge: Cambridge University Press.

———— (1993) "Trotsky and the Wild Orchids." *Common Knowledge* 1 (3): 140–53.

———— (1995) "Two Cheers for Elitism." *New Yorker* (January 30).

———— (1998) *Achieving Our Country: Leftist Thought in Twentieth-Century America.* Cambridge, Mass.: Harvard University Press.

Rosen, Gary (1999) *American Compact: James Madison and the Problem of Founding.* Lawrence: University Press of Kansas.

Rossum, Ralph, and McDowell, Gary L., eds. (1981) *The American Founding: Politics, Statesmanship, and the Constitution.* Port Washington, N.Y.: Kennikat Press.

Ruderman, Richard S. (1997a) "Aristotle and the Recovery of Political Judgment." *American Political Science Review* 91 (2): 409–20.

———— (1997b) "Democracy and the Problem of Statesmanship." *Review of Politics* 59 (4): 759–87.

———— (2002) "Political Judgment in Dark Times: Frederick Douglass and Slavery." In Ethan Fishman, ed., *"Phronesis": Studies in the Nature and Scope of Prudential Leadership.* Lanham, Md.: Lexington Press.

———— (2003) " 'Proclaim Liberty Throughout the Land': Frederick Douglass, William Lloyd Garrison, and the Abolition of Slavery." In Frost and Sikkenga, 2003.

Ruderman, Richard S., and Godwin, R. Kenneth (2000) "Liberalism and Parental Control of Education." *Review of Politics* 62: 503–29.

Rush, Myron (1958) *The Rise of Khrushchev.* Washington: Public Affairs Press.

———— (1965) *Political Succession in the USSR.* New York: Columbia University Press.

———— (1974) *How Communist States Change Their Rulers.* Ithaca: Cornell University Press.

———— (1993) "Fortune and Fate." *National Interest* 31: 19–25.

Sabine, George (1953) Review of *Persecution and the Art of Writing,* in *Ethics* 63: 220–22.

Salkever, Stephen G. (1987) "The Crisis of Liberal Democracy: Liberality and Democratic Citizenship." In Kenneth L. Deutsch and Walter Soffer, eds., *The Crisis of Liberal Democracy.* Albany: SUNY Press.

———— (1990) *Finding the Mean: Theory and Practice in Aristotelian Political Philosophy.* Princeton: Princeton University Press.

———— (1991) "Aristotle's Social Science." In Carnes Lord and David K. O'Connor, eds., *Essays on the Foundations of Aristotelian Political Science.* Berkeley: University of California Press.

Sartori, Giovanni, Laitin, David D., and Colomer, Joseph M. (2004) "Symposium: Where is Political Science Going?" *PS: Political Science and Politics* 37: 785–94.

Schaub, Diana (2000) "The Spirit of a Free Man." *Public Interest* 140: 86–107.

Schramm, Peter W., and Wilson, Bradford P., eds. (1993) *American Political Parties and Constitutional Politics.* Lanham, Md.: Rowman & Littlefield.

Schwartz, Joel (1990) "Freud and the American Constitution." In Bloom, 1990a.

———— (2000) *Fighting Poverty with Virtue: Moral Reform and America's Urban Poor, 1825–2000.* Bloomington: Indiana University Press.

Shell, Susan (1990) "Idealism." In Bloom, 1990a.

Shulsky, Abram (1991a) "The 'Infrastructure' of Aristotle's *Politics:* Aristotle on Economics and Politics." In Carnes Lord and David K. O'Connor, eds., *Essays on the Foundations of Aristotelian Political Science.* Berkeley: University of California Press.

———— (1991b) *Silent Warfare: Understanding the World of Intelligence.* Washington: Brassey's/Macmillan.

Stauffer, Devin (2001) *Plato's Introduction to the Question of Justice.* Albany: SUNY Press.

———— (2006) *The Unity of Plato's "Gorgias": Rhetoric, Justice, and the Philosophic Life.* Cambridge: Cambridge University Press.

Stavely, Richard W. (1972) "Political Economy Ancient and Modern: Aristotle, Locke, and Keynes." In D. P. Crook, ed., *Questioning the Past.* St. Lucia, Australia: University of Queensland Press.

Stavely, Richard W., and Vinnicombe, Thea (2002) "John Locke, Thomas Hobbes, and the Development of Political Economy." *International Journal of Social Economics* 29 (9): 690–705.

Stevens, Richard (1997) *The American Constitution and Its Provenance.* Lanham, Md.: Rowman & Littlefield.

Stoner, James R., Jr. (1994) *Common Law and Liberal Theory: Coke, Hobbes, and the Origins of American Constitutionalism.* Lawrence: University Press of Kansas.

——— (1998) "The Idiom of Common Law in the Formation of Judicial Power." In Bradford P. Wilson and Ken Masugi, eds., *The Supreme Court and American Constitutionalism.* Lanham, Md.: Rowman & Littlefield.

——— (2003) *Common Law Liberty: Rethinking American Constitutionalism.* Lawrence: University Press of Kansas.

Storing, Herbert J., ed. (1962) *Essays on the Scientific Study of Politics.* New York: Holt, Rinehart and Winston.

——— (1964) "The Crucial Link: Public Administration, Responsibility, and the Public Interest." *Public Administration Review* 24 (1): 39–46. (Reprinted in *Toward a More Perfect Union.*)

——— (1980) "American Statesmanship Old and New." In Robert A. Goldwin, ed., *Bureaucrats, Policy Analysts, Statesmen: Who Leads?* Washington: AEI Press. (Reprinted in *Toward a More Perfect Union.*)

———, ed. (1981) *The Complete Anti-Federalist.* 7 vols. Chicago: University of Chicago Press.

——— (1995) *Toward a More Perfect Union.* Ed. Joseph M. Bessette. Washington: AEI Press.

Storing, Herbert J., and Self, Peter (1963) *The State and the Farmer: British Agricultural Policies and Politics.* Berkeley: University of California Press.

Strahan, Randall (1990) *New Ways and Means: Reform and Change in a Congressional Committee.* Chapel Hill: University of North Carolina Press.

Strauss, Leo (1936) *The Political Philosophy of Hobbes: Its Basis and Its Genesis.* Trans. Elsa M. Sinclair. Oxford: Clarendon Press.

——— (1946) "On a New Interpretation of Plato's Political Philosophy." *Social Research* 13: 326–67.

——— (1952a) "On Collingwood's Philosophy of History." *Review of Metaphysics* 5 (June): 559–86.

——— (1952b) *Persecution and the Art of Writing.* Glencoe, Ill.: Free Press.

———— (1953) *Natural Right and History*. Chicago: University of Chicago Press.

———— (1958) *Thoughts on Machiavelli*. Glencoe, Ill.: Free Press.

———— (1959) *What Is Political Philosophy?* Glencoe, Ill.: Free Press.

———— (1964) *The City and Man*. Chicago: Rand McNally.

———— (1965a) *Hobbes' politische Wissenschaft*. Neuweid am Rhein: Hermann Luchterland. Republished in vol. 3 of the *Gesammalte Schriften*.

———— (1965b) *Spinoza's Critique of Religion*. Trans. Elsa M. Sinclair. New York: Schocken.

———— (1966) *Socrates and Aristophanes*. New York: Basic Books.

———— (1968) *Liberalism Ancient and Modern*. New York: Basic Books.

———— (1975) *The Argument and the Action of Plato's "Laws."* Chicago: University of Chicago Press.

———— (1979) "Preface to *Hobbes' politische Wissenschaft*." In *Interpretation: A Journal of Political Philosophy* 8 (January): 1–3, a translation, by Donald Maletz, of the Preface to the book published at Neuweid am Rhein: Hermann Luchterland, 1965.

———— (1983) *Studies in Platonic Political Philosophy*. Chicago: University of Chicago Press.

———— (1987) *History of Political Philosophy*. Ed. Leo Strauss and Joseph Cropsey, 3rd ed. Chicago: University of Chicago Press.

———— (1989a) *The Rebirth of Classical Political Rationalism*. Chicago: University of Chicago Press.

———— (1989b) "Three Waves of Modernity." In Hilail Gilden, ed., *An Introduction to Political Philosophy: Ten Essays by Leo Strauss*. Detroit: Wayne State University Press.

———— (1991) *On Tyranny*. Revised and expanded edition. New York: Free Press.

———— (1995) *Philosophy and Law*. Albany: SUNY Press; a translation, by Eve Adler, of *Philosophie und Gesetz*, originally published in 1935 and republished in vol. 2 of the *Gesammelte Schriften*.

———— (1996–) *Gesammelte Schriften*. Ed. Heinrich Meier, 3 vols. thus far. Stuttgart: J. B. Metzler.

Strauss, Leo, and Kojève, Alexandre (1991) *On Tyranny,* rev. ed. New York: Free Press. (Orig. pub. 1948.)

Sullivan, Vickie B. (1996) "Machiavelli's Momentary 'Machiavellian

Moment': A Reconsideration of Pocock's Treatment of the *Discourses.*" *Political Theory* 20: 25–44.

——— (2004) *Machiavelli, Hobbes, and the Formation of a Liberal Republicanism in England.* Cambridge: Cambridge University Press.

Taft, William Howard (1916) *Our Chief Magistrate and His Powers.* New York: Columbia University Press.

Tarcov, Nathan (1982a) "Political Thought in Early Modern Europe II: The Age of Reformation." *Journal of Modern History* 54: 56–65.

——— (1982b) "Quentin Skinner's Method and Machiavelli's *Prince.*" *Ethics* 92: 692–709.

——— (1983a) "A 'Non-Lockean' Locke and the Character of Liberalism." In Douglas MacLean and Claudia Mills, eds., *Liberalism Reconsidered.* Lanham, Md.: Rowman & Allanheld.

——— (1983b) "Philosophy and History: Tradition and Interpretation in the Work of Leo Strauss." *Polity* 16 (1): 5–29.

——— (1984) *Locke's Education for Liberty.* Chicago: University of Chicago Press.

——— (1988) "The Spirit of Liberty and Early American Foreign Policy." In Catherine Zuckert, ed., *Understanding the Political Spirit: Philosophical Investigation from Socrates to Nietzsche.* New Haven: Yale University Press.

——— (1989a) "If This Long War Is Over." *National Interest* 18: 50–53.

——— (1989b) "Principle and Prudence: The Use of Force from the Founders' Perspective." In Fred E. Baumann and Kenneth M. Jensen, eds., *American Defense Policy and Liberal Democracy.* Charlottesville: University Press of Virginia.

——— (1990) "Principle, Prudence, and the Constitutional Division of Foreign Policy." In Goldwin and Licht, 1990.

——— (1991) "On a Certain Critique of 'Straussianism.'" *Review of Politics* 53: 3–18.

Tatalovich, Raymond (1995) *Nativism Reborn?: The Official English Language Movement and the American States.* Lexington: University Press of Kentucky.

——— (2000) "George Washington: The First Modern President? A Reply to Nichols." In Mark J. Rozell, William Pederson, and Frank J. Williams, eds., *George Washington and the Origins of the American Presidency.* Westport, Conn.: Praeger.

Tatalovich, Raymond, and Engeman, Thomas S., eds. (2003). *The Presidency and Political Science: Two Hundred Years of Constitutional Debate.* Baltimore: Johns Hopkins University Press.

Tessitore, Aristide (2002) "Alexis de Tocqueville on the Natural State of Religion in the Age of Democracy." *Journal of Politics* 64: 1137–52.

Thompson, C. Bradley (1998a) *John Adams and the Spirit of Liberty.* Lawrence: University Press of Kansas.

——— (1998b) "Young John Adams and the New Philosophic Rationalism." *William and Mary Quarterly,* 3rd series, 55: 259–80.

Thompson, Norma (2001) *The Ship of State: Statecraft and Politics from Ancient Greece to Democratic America.* New Haven: Yale University Press.

Tulis, Jeffrey (1987) *The Rhetorical Presidency.* Princeton: Princeton University Press.

——— (1991a) "Comment: Riker's Rhetoric of Ratification." *Studies in American Political Development* 5: 284–92.

——— (1991b) "The Constitution of American Political Development and the Modern Presidency." In Martin Fausold and Alan Shank, eds., *The Presidency and the Constitution.* Albany: SUNY Press.

Uhr, John (1998) *Deliberative Democracy in Australia: The Changing Place of Parliament.* Cambridge: Cambridge University Press.

Verba, Sidney, Schlozman, Kay L., and Brady, Henry E. (2000) "Rational Action and Political Activity." *Journal of Theoretical Politics* 12: 243–68.

Waltz, Kenneth (1959) *Man, the State, and War.* New York: Columbia University Press.

——— (1979) *Theory of International Politics.* New York: McGraw-Hill.

Walzer, Michael (1977) *Just and Unjust Wars: A Moral Argument with Historical Illustrations.* New York: Basic Books.

Weinstein, Leo (1962) "The Group Approach: Arthur F. Bentley." In Storing, 1962.

Wilson, Bradford P., and Schramm, Peter W., eds. (1994) *Separation of Powers and Good Government.* Lanham, Md.: Rowman & Littlefield.

Wilson, James Q. (1985a) *Crime and Human Nature.* New York: Simon and Schuster.

——— (1985b) "The Rediscovery of Character: Private Virtue and Public Policy." *Public Interest* 81: 3–16.

———— (1990) "Interests and Deliberation in the American Republic, or, Why James Madison Would Never Have Received the James Madison Award." *PS: Political Science and Politics* 23: 4.

———— (1993) "The Moral Sense." *American Political Science Review* 87: 1–11.

———— (1995) *On Character,* expanded ed. Washington: AEI Press.

———— (2002) *The Marriage Problem: How Our Culture Has Weakened Families.* New York: HarperCollins.

Wilson, Woodrow (1908) *Constitutional Government.* New York: Columbia University Press.

Winthrop, Delba (1986) "Tocqueville's American Woman and 'The True Conception of Democratic Progress.'" *Political Theory* 14: 239–61.

———— (1992) "Comments on Stephen Schneck's Reading of Tocqueville." *Polity* 25: 299–306.

Wirls, Daniel, and Wirls, Stephen (2004) *The Invention of the United States Senate.* Baltimore: Johns Hopkins University Press.

Wolfe, Christopher (1979) "Woodrow Wilson: Interpreting the Constitution." *Review of Politics* 41: 121–42.

———— (1986) *The Rise of Modern Judicial Review.* New York: Basic Books.

———— (1996) *How to Read the Constitution: Originalism, Constitutional Interpretation, and Judicial Power.* Lanham, Md.: Rowman & Littlefield.

Wood, Gordon S. (1972) *The Creation of the American Republic, 1776–1787.* New York: Norton.

Yarbrough, Jean (1991) "Race and the Moral Foundation of the American Republic: Another Look at the Declaration and the *Notes on Virginia.*" *Journal of Politics* 53 (1): 90–105.

———— (1998) *American Virtues: Thomas Jefferson on the Character of a Free People.* Lawrence: University Press of Kansas.

Zetterbaum, Marvin (1967) *Tocqueville and the Problem of Democracy.* Stanford: Stanford University Press.

Zuckert, Catherine H. (1995) "On the Rationality of Rational Choice." *Political Psychology* 16 (1): 179–98.

Zuckert, Michael P. (1981) "Liberalism and Nihilism: Contemporary Constrained Performance Theories of Justice." *Constitutional Commentary* 2 (2): 389–417.

———— (1986) "Congressional Power under the Fourteenth Amendment." *Constitutional Commentary* 3: 123–55.

———— (1987) "Completing the Constitution: The Thirteenth Amendment." *Constitutional Commentary* 4: 259–83.

———— (1990) "The Federalist at 200—What's It to Us?" *Constitutional Commentary* 7: 97–107.

———— (1993) Review of Earl M. Malz, *Civil Rights, the Constitution, and Congress, 1863–1869. Constitutional Commentary* 10: 266–72.

———— (1994a) *Natural Rights and the New Republicanism.* Princeton: Princeton University Press.

———— (1994b) "The New Rawls and Constitutional Theory: Does It Really Taste that Much Better?" *Constitutional Commentary* 11: 227–45.

———— (1996) *The Natural Rights Republic: Studies in the Foundation of the American Political Tradition.* Notre Dame: University of Notre Dame Press.

———— (1998) "Fundamental Rights, the Supreme Court and American Constitutionalism: The Lessons of the Civil Rights Act of 1866." In Bradford P. Wilson and Ken Masugi, eds., *The Supreme Court and American Constitutionalism.* Lanham, Md.: Rowman & Littlefield.

———— (1999) "Refinding the Founding: Martin Diamond, Leo Strauss, and the American Regime." In Kenneth L. Deutsch and John A. Murley, eds., *Leo Strauss, the Straussians, and the American Regime.* Lanham, Md.: Rowman & Littlefield.

———— (2001) "Pride and Political Philosophy." *Claremont Review of Books* 1 (4): 17, 23.

———— (2002) *Launching Liberalism: On Lockean Political Philosophy.* Lawrence: University Press of Kansas.

Zvesper, John (1977) *Political Philosophy and Rhetoric: A Study of the Origins of American Party Politics.* Cambridge: Cambridge University Press.

———— (1984) "The Madisonian Systems." *Western Political Quarterly* 37: 236–56.

Index

Abbreviations of works by Strauss are keyed to the list in "Notes."

Wilson, Bradford, 148n23, 150n45
Wilson, James Q., 146n6, 152nn54, 57
Wilson, Woodrow, 113–14, 116
Winthrop, Delba, 147n10, 152n54
Wirls, Daniel, 148n23
Wirls, Stephen, 148n23
Wolfe, Christopher, 149n30, 150n37
Wood, Gordon, 153n60

Xenophon, 37, 39, 51, 65–66, 141n5, 145n2; *Education of Cyrus,* 141n5; *Memorabilia,* 66, 142n10

Yarbrough, Jean, 152nn52, 54

Zetterbaum, Marvin, 152n53
Zinman, Richard, 152n54
Zuckert, Catherine, 146n6
Zuckert, Michael, 125, 144n19, 146n5, 148n23, 149n30, 151n51, 153n62
Zvesper, John, 148n23, 151n47